Adopting in China:

A Practical Guide/
an Emotional Journey

By Kathleen Wheeler, Ph.D. and Doug Werner
Photography by Doug Werner

Tracks Publishing
Chula Vista, California

TRACKS
PUBLISHING

Adopting in China:
A Practical Guide/
an Emotional Journey

By Kathleen Wheeler, Ph.D. and Doug Werner

Tracks Publishing
140 Brightwood Avenue
Chula Vista, CA 91910
619-476-7125 Fax 619-476-8173

Publisher's Cataloging in Publication

Werner, Doug, 1950-
    Adopting in China : a practical guide/an
emotional journey / by Doug Werner ; edited by
Kathleen Wheeler ; photography by Doug Werner.–
1st ed.
    p. cm.
    Includes bibliographical references and index.
    LCCN: 99-75647
    ISBN: 1-884654-00-2

    1. Intercountry adoption–China.
    2.Intercountry adoption–United States.
    I. Title.

HV875.58.C6W43 1999   362.7'34
                      QBI99-1425

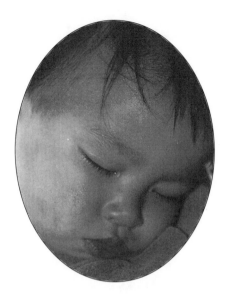

The Chinese called our child Lucky One
because she had found a home with us.

This book is dedicated to all the Lucky Ones
in our group and all the Lucky Ones-to-Be
waiting for families to take them home.

Acknowledgements:

Norma Caro

China Team:
Norman
Sarah
Grace
Lucy
Rachel
Martin

Family Connections Adoptions
Sandie Hicks
Nancy Cowie

Adoption Services International
Norma Fulkerson

Phyllis Carter
Phyllis Levitt
Bob Smith
Jeanne Lindsay
Ann Werner
Red Werner
Genie Wheeler
Gene Wheeler

China Groups 21 and 22:
All 24 families

Contents

Introduction   7

1. Four Decisions   9
2. Costs   21
3. It Can Be Done! Adoption Procedure   35
4. Preparing for a New Life   47
5. Being There: A Journal of Our Trip to China   57
6. The New Life   105
7. One Year Later   117

Appendix: What Other Adoptive Parents Think   121

Glossary   133
Resources   135
Bibliography   140
Index   141

First romp with a hose (June 1999).

Introduction

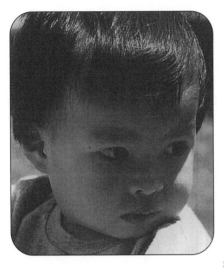

This book is intended to give those considering adopting in China a brief overview of what we went through to find our daughter Joy.

It is our hope that our reflections and experiences will help people gain a better understanding of what Chinese adoption is all about. So much seems to be shrouded in mystery, red tape and, at times, misinformation. Make no mistake — it's very important to have faith as you plunge ahead with your decision, but it's also nice to have a little down-to-earth information from folks who have been there.

Please keep in mind that this is just one couple's adoption story. There is no guarantee that the experience will be the same for others. However, since we used qualified adoption services available to everyone and have been absolutely candid about everything, it should serve well as a reliable reference.

Best of luck to those of you who choose to adopt in China. The adoption experience will no doubt be one of the most remarkable in your life. The sometimes grinding process will reintroduce you to yourself, the trip to China will open your mind, and the somewhat rumpled child you take in will literally bloom before your eyes.

It's an emotional roller coaster, sure. But more importantly for us, it's been an emotional *training program* — you start out with a heart this big and end up with one the size of the universe.

Doug Werner
Kathleen Wheeler/ Werner
& Joy Werner

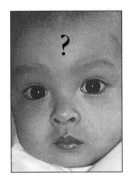

Chapter One:
Four Decisions

There were four very important decisions to make about our adoption that required careful consideration. We've listed them here to help you think through your own situation. Since the process is intensely personal, you will, of course, eventually arrive at your decisions in your own way.

1. To have a child or not

Do you *really want a child?* Couples may discover that one of them may be more motivated than the other, but ultimately both people must desire to be parents. This decision is a snap for some and a longer process for others. Those on the fence about having children (as we were for so long) may wonder:

● What if we* find we don't like having a child once we have one?

● Are we willing to give up our freedom and lifestyle?

*We're not discriminating against single parents! In this case the subject should read We/I in order to be sensitive to all prospective parents. However this kind of indication is awkward and annoying to read throughout the entire book. Let it be known that single persons are certainly invited to the party (and can make good parents) but for the sake of easy reading, we'll be sticking to slash-less pronouns.

● Do we want to spend the money that's required?

● Are we willing to make career sacrifices?

● Can we deal with dirty diapers, crying and runny noses every day?

There's a lot of this ...

Kathleen and I lingered over these and other questions for years. Our leaning, stumbling and running toward parenthood was long, gradual and fairly steady. We decided to have a child when it looked like time was running out (we were both 46), and when we felt we had enough financial security. We had enjoyed the freedom of a childless life for a long time and we wanted to experience parenthood.

The ball started to roll when Kathleen decided she really wanted a kid. As for me, I always liked children and began to enjoy the idea of being a daddy, but I didn't share her sense of urgency. To be honest, I sort of wafted along with the preparations my wife made. My connection to this thing grew over time and probably didn't cement until Joy was in my arms.

Plans gradually took form without serious doubt and

with an increasing sense of joyful anticipation. Finally, we woke one morning on a jet speeding over the Pacific and realized we were committed. Except for a few frustrated and superheated moments, we have never really, I mean *really*, regretted the choice. After a year or so, Joy has become the center of our universe and we have strong faith that she will remain so until she brings home her first surly teenage boyfriend.

Sure, we miss going to the movies, quiet dinners and reading the newspaper without interruption. I miss surfing at 6 a.m., working until 7 p.m. and being able to hear the TV. We don't like loaded diapers, tantrums or mucus any more than we imagined we would, but it doesn't bother us all that much. You get used to it. It gets better.

Like doubt used to, belief in parenthood grows all by itself. People in our lives are happy for us. The kid is surprisingly entertaining. She's a lot of fun! Our lives have filled out. It continues to feel like the right thing.

Years ago I asked a friend with young children if he ever had second thoughts about having them. Did he ever feel stuck in a life he can't easily leave for several more years? He looked at me and laughed. *They're my kids!* he said. *They're just ... my kids.*

Now I know what he means.

2.Adopting a child
(versus giving birth)
Like I said, Kathleen and I were each 46 when we

decided that we *both* wanted to be parents. Today there are options that include birthing for middle-aged women. Although we gave it some thought, we didn't like the idea or the chances or the *chancy-ness* of having our own baby. I did not want her to go through pregnancy with or without drugs or medical procedures. Actually, neither of us held a strong desire to create a child in the first place. We honestly felt that there was a child out there, somewhere, meant for us.

There are good reasons to adopt and some not so good reasons. This list from Adoption Services International (ASI) may be helpful to those considering adoption.

Good reasons:
● You want to know the joy of helping a child grow up to be a happy and fulfilled adult.

● You have a strong desire to provide love and care for a child.

● You really like children and want to add one to your family.

● You want to be someone's parent.

Not so good reasons *(with rejoinders)*:
● You want a playmate for your birth child.
Better to hire a neighbor's child.

● Your religion tells you to reach out.
So put a big donation in the collection plate.

● Your infertility is a constant sadness.
Adopting doesn't cure it.

● You are affluent and could give so much.
Write a check to charity.

● Your marriage is shaky and a child might help.
It'll never happen.

● Since we can't have birth children, we might as well adopt.
Get past the notion of second best.

● You feel so empty. A child will help.
Find a friend.

● You pity those poor children.
No child needs pity.

Our reasons were probably a little of both:
● After bouncing back and forth for years, Kathleen finally bounced forth. I think that's a reason by itself. Call it momentum.

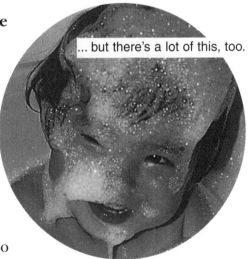

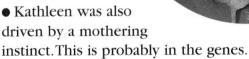
... but there's a lot of this, too.

● Kathleen was also driven by a mothering instinct. This is probably in the genes.

● I went along with it because Kathleen really wanted it this time.

● If we didn't adopt now, then when would we ever do it? Call it not wanting to miss out.

● I also liked the idea of having a little one call me Daddy. Maybe that's in my genes.

● It felt nice and it felt right. Aw shucks.

● I did not want Kathleen to give birth at 46.

Joy waiting it out in the Yang Dong Orphanage — about a month before we came.

● We honestly felt that there was a child out there waiting for us.

3.Adopting internationally
(versus the U.S.)

Adoption in this country was out of the question because of our desire to have a healthy, younger child. By and large, we were too old for that. We did not want to adopt a child with major health or emotional problems. We did not want to adopt a child older than three years. We did not want to deal with the whims of a surrogate or birth mother. We had to look across the borders and that was OK with us. We had no reservations about adopting a child from another nation.

4. Adopting from China (versus other countries)

Kathleen studied the availability of children in several countries and liked what she saw in China. Various sources said that there were up to four million baby girls in orphanages. This is due to a government policy prohibiting having more than two children per family, coupled with the traditional Chinese preference for male offspring — not because they dislike girls, but because boys are raised to provide for their elders and carry on the family name (see sidebar).

We learned that couples from outside China could adopt healthy, abuse-free children up to 45 years younger than themselves. As a rule, Chinese orphans do not suffer from the effects of drug-plagued, alcoholic or abusive environments. They are often perfectly normal baby girls abandoned by parents forced to do so by a government trying to limit population growth and a culture that makes it imperative to have a boy.

I fancied the thought of China — mysterious and exotic (to us) and far, far away. I also liked the idea of adopting a girl because I enjoyed the notion of a single-bull household (no battling over the drumstick at Thanksgiving, for example). Kathleen wanted a girl all along. Perfect.

Why are there so many Chinese girls in orphanages?

In 1979 the Chinese government initiated a one-child-per-family policy in order to curb population growth. It was loosely enforced because such a drastic measure was met with resistance by the people. Like folks anywhere, the Chinese wanted to raise families without interference. The one-child policy also put those families who did not conceive a male child at a severe disadvantage.

This is because sons play a very important social and economic function in China, especially in the tradition-bound rural areas. Sons care and provide for family elders, since there is no pension system in China. So, despite the policy, families kept trying to produce sons and attempted to hide daughters through informal adoptions within family structures.

In response, the government initiated a one-son/two-child policy that was and is strictly enforced. A family now may have a second child if the first is not a boy, but they must stop conceiving after that or face severe penalty. The government also cracked down on domestic adoptions so families could no longer hide daughters with relatives.

Those who violate the one-son/two child policy are forced into a great bind. Punishment includes a fine that most families cannot afford. Parents cannot place a child for adoption unless they are destitute. By taking a child to an orphanage, parents could be admitting to violating the policy. In fact, anyone who brings a child to officials is questioned about parentage.

This only encourages people to abandon baby girls and discourages anybody who finds them from notifying the authorities. Often this means that by the time officials find the baby, the child's life may be in danger.

Like so many children, our Joy was carefully abandoned early in the day and placed at the steps of a government building. Officials discovered her quickly and placed her in proper care. We think of the mother and the decision she felt she had to make. We have kept her Chinese name, Xiao Rou, as a middle name to honor the birth mother and her sacrifice.

Kathleen's Decision
As a little girl I never questioned that I would have a child some day. Throughout my adolescence and college years I spent many happy hours with children — babysitting, volunteering in a pediatrics ward and working with disturbed children. Then my life took a different turn. After I turned 21, I spent very little time with children.

At 46, I thought I was at peace with not having a child. Over the years I had wrestled with the reality of finding myself in a life where circumstances never quite led in that direction. I always had firm criteria for having a child — I wanted a partner, I wanted a partner who wanted children as much as I did, and I wanted to know that I had sufficient resources (time, energy and money) to share with a child and to give her a good life.

The partner requirement took me until I was 40 — I had several disappointments in love in my 20s and 30s. When I met Doug at 36, we were both working hard at the business of making a  living. He wasn't interested in having children at the time, and I admit I was reluctant to take a detour from a career that demanded my full attention. As the years passed, I was mostly grateful to have a close companion in my life, let alone a family. At 40, we married and I thought I was willing to accept a life without children. However, the desire to parent did not leave me, and when Doug changed his mind and was willing to adopt, the possibility of fulfilling the dream suddenly became real.

I was also terrified. I had listened to many women talk about their struggles balancing children and career and I knew it would be difficult. I was especially loathe to lose sleep. I was barely beginning to feel truly successful at my chosen field. Perhaps job confidence comes easily to others, but it has been hard-won for me. My job has always consumed me and I wondered how I could fit a child in. I was also fearful that my reasons for wanting a child were all wrong and that perhaps I was even asking too much of life. I worried that

I wanted more than I had the resources to manage. Would I have enough — enough time, energy and financial resources to give her?

What made me take the final plunge was the thought that anything is better than an orphanage. Whatever mistakes we make, whatever limitations we might have as parents, at least we would be giving her a loving home and a *chance* at a good life. With this thought in mind, I made our first appointment with Sandie Hicks of Family Connections Adoptions in Oceanside, California.

The decision was not made all at once, and unlike many other parents, single or married, we have had periodic spasms of ambivalence. It was enormously helpful to talk with other parents (especially those our age and older) and learn about their experiences. Their stories included a consistent refrain — *it is more work and more joy than we ever imagined.* Not one family said that they regretted their decision. I talked with nearly 40 people, including couples and single mothers (and one single father) who had gone through the process and who were thrilled with their child and with the experience of being parents. Although I was nervous about the "more work" part of their tune, I was filled with excitement about the "more joy" possibility.

During one conversation with a valued mentor in my life, I asked, "What do you think is the best reason not to do this and what is the best reason to do it?" Her reply said it all, "The best reason not to do it is that it will stretch you significantly and you may become overwhelmed. The best reason to do it is that you will have a child to love." She was right.

I knew I would have to give up expensive vacations, a bigger house, a better car and other nice things I'd love to have. I may have to work past age 65 or even 70 (my own parents are great role models since they continue to work at 75 and 80!). But I wanted to love and nurture someone outside myself. It meant something to me to give a loving home to a child. Armed with that motivation, we embarked on the long journey that continues today.

Chapter Two:
Costs

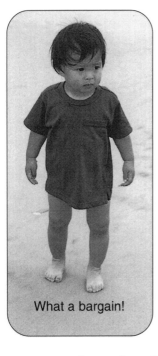

What a bargain!

Our adoption cost $17,294.*
The last time we spent that
much money we had bought a
new car (*that* will tell you
something about yourself —
car or kid?)

At first I was suspicious.
Seventeen grand is a lot of
money. If the problem is too
many orphans (like *four million* too many), why not airlift
the kids to the United States?
Loving and suitable parents are
waiting in line. After all, it is a humanitarian problem
and these folks appear to be *selling their kids*, for
God's sake.

I've since modified my position considerably. The agencies, courts, orphanages, heck, even the governments
employ good, hard-working people that should be paid
for the work they do. I also discovered that the Chinese
love their little girls and that my initial view was much
too harsh. Living is difficult over there and the problems of overpopulation aren't easy to comprehend and
solve. The price tag looks fairly reasonable now.

*Of course, this cost represents only the beginning. Raising a
child, by some estimates, costs $750,000 over the course of
21 years. Prospective parents are wise to think about that. But
perhaps not too hard.

Fees for our adoption

This is what the adoption cost us. There are a number of variables that affect fees and your fees will no doubt be different. However, in the spirit of candor we felt it was important to reveal our bill. There's entirely too much speculation surrounding this subject and it contributes to the mystery of adoption. Hard numbers help make solid decisions.

1. Family Connections Adoption Agency

Homestudy reports	$ 1550
Re-adopt (obtaining a U.S. birth certificate) and post-placement visit	$ 700
California homestudy fingerprint processing	$ 150
Family Connections total	**$ 2400**

2. Immigration and Naturalization Service (INS)

I-600 (Application for Advanced Processing of Orphan Petition)	$ 405
INS fingerprint processing ($25 per person)	$ 50
INS total	**$ 455**

3. Ho Ho Travel (airline tickets) — **$ 1567**

4. China Youth Travel Service (hotels and meals in China) — **$ 2780**

5. Chinese Government, orphanage and U.S. Consulate

Donation to orphanage	$ 3000
Donation to caretaker of orphanage	$ 150
Adoption Certificate from local Civil Affairs Office	$ 100
Government Notary Office	$ 550
Passport office under the Public Security Bureau	$ 150
Ministry of Civil Affairs in Beijing	$ 465
Medical checkup/Four photos of child	$ 40

U.S. Consulate/Child's U.S. Immigrant Visa	$ 325
Airport construction fee (airport tax)	$ 12
Chinese Government, orphanage and U.S. Consulate total	**$ 4792**
6. **Our international child program***	**$ 4800**
7. **Miscellaneous expenses (tips, gifts, gas, meals, etc.)**	**$ 500**
Grand total	**$17294**

Explaining the fees

1. Family Connections: $2400
This sum paid for the homestudy required by California state law that included four visits and interviews by a certified social worker. This state-licensed adoption agency helped with all the necessary paperwork and arrangements required by state and federal law including post-placement visits and reports, fingerprint processing, re-adopt and obtaining a California state birth certificate. (The term *re-adopt* is used because the child already underwent an official Chinese adoption — an adoption in the United States is therefore a *re-adoption*.)

> *Our international child program asked that we not use their name in the text (we could, however, use photos). Their reasons are somewhat mysterious (something about the Chinese government) but of course, that's their business. This is unfortunate because we very much want to tell the world about their superior program.

2. Ho Ho Travel (airline tickets): $1567
(Paid through our child program.)
This covered flight arrangements to China from Los
Angeles and back. This is the cost of two round-trip
economy class tickets and included the child's fare for
the flight back. Business class was an option. Although
it was quite a bit more expensive, it did allow those
who chose it to fly back with a great deal more comfort. (Most of us gutted it out in economy class and it
was indeed hellish.)

**3. Immigration and
Naturalization Service
(INS): $455**
These are fees for application
and fingerprint processing.
(This fingerprint processing is
different from the homestudy
processing.)

**4. China Youth
Travel Service
(hotels and meals in
China): $2780**
(Paid through our
child program.)
This amount covered:

China Hotel was first-class
comfort all the way in stark
contrast with the teeming
urban life surrounding it.

A. Eight and one half nights at
the China Hotel in Guangzhou and two nights at
Yangjiang International Hotel in Yang Dong. They were
both first-class accommodations. The China Hotel is a
five-star hotel and the Yangjiang International Hotel is
not far behind.

We were not allowed inside the orphanage, but caretakers that we met seemed very dedicated and caring.

B. Ten western breakfasts, six Chinese lunches and ten Chinese dinners. All meals were served in the hotels or in first-class restaurants.

C. Transportation to various offices and orphanage. This included an eight-hour, round-trip bus ride to the town where the orphanage is and several short trips for adoption business.

D. Numerous sight-seeing and shopping tours in Guangzhou.

5. Chinese Government, orphanage and U.S. Consulate: $4792
This price included the $3000 donation to the orphanage, which seemed sort of suspect for the amount and the word "donation." But apparently these donations are a cornerstone of support for Chinese orphanages. There is little or no government support for child welfare in China.

6. International child program: $4800
This is the child program that found Joy for us. They were our "Chinese Connection." Our child program was made up of several people (called "China Team") who lived and traveled with us for the entire visit (you cannot travel on your own in China — you need a child program approved by the Chinese government to handle the details of your adoption and stay).

Without the can-do professionals of China Team, we would still be there. Thank you, ladies. From left: Rachel, Lucy, Kathleen and Joy, Grace, and Sarah.

The China Team met us at the airport and gently dictated our every move until we boarded our flight back to Los Angeles. They safeguarded our money, arranged for doctors (fees included) and stood over our shoulders and told us what to say and write before Chinese officials.* They taught us how to make baby formula, how to sing Chinese lullabies, what China was all about for the last 30 years and gave hands-on counsel for every baby (and parent) need 24 hours a day. We were astounded and so very gratified by their call to duty. We will never forget them.

*Half of the $4800 fee goes toward the intricate and rather daunting task of documentation. Our child program took care of it all: translation, notarization and authentication. They also coordinated the child referral with the Chinese government and the family. It should be noted that not all child programs provide such complete services. Families who have to procure documentation themselves face a great deal of red tape.

Trip and Post-trip costs

In order to present a more comprehensive report on costs for adding a child to a household budget, here's a breakdown of baby and parent needs and supplies for the trip itself and for day-to-day costs immediately thereafter.

Trip costs (preparations)

$250 max. (Assuming you already have camera and/or camcorder and only need film, batteries or cassettes.) This sum should cover the following items:

Formula

Formula is the white powdered substance that is mixed with warm water for your baby's bottle. It's made of dried milk, soy beans and/or rice. Kids use a bottle for up to two years. Formula may be provided by your child program on your trip. Otherwise, an $18 tin of formula is more than enough for 10 days. It also comes in convenient single-serving packets.

Bottles and nipples

Most babies in China are used to Evenflo or Gerber nipples. They are also used to a very thick formula mixture that requires a large nipple hole. Bring a knife or scissors to enlarge the nipple opening.

Bottle brush for cleaning

This is especially necessary if the formula has dried inside the bottle.

Thermos

A small (pint) thermos enables you to carry very hot

water on your many bus trips in China. You mix the hot water with bottled water to get the right temperature.

Baby food and spoon
Necessary if your child is old enough to handle solid food. Baby cereal is best.

Pacifiers (2)
Can really live up to its name.

Diapers
Babies need to be changed 5-7 times a day. So you'll need 50-70 diapers for a ten-day trip. A pack of 68 costs $18.

Ziplock bags
Bring all sizes. The gallon size are good to stash used diapers when on the run.

Baby wipes
You'll need more wipes than diapers. One wipe will do for each pee change, but you'll need more for the other, for sure. Five bucks buys a pack of 68.

Diaper rash cream
Diaper rash is a common malady. Joy got it and her tiny groin area looked like it had been painted with day-glo magenta paint. There are a number of over-the-counter brands. We swear by Aveeno.

Pediatric syringe
This is for giving liquid medication by mouth.

Dimetapp
... for a runny nose. Use also for decongesting baby's ears for the return flight. Give to your child 30 minutes before departure and landing.

Pedialyte
... for diarrhea

Baby Tylenol
... for pain and fever.

Baby thermometer

Baby nasal aspirator
This is a squeezable rubber ball with nasal insert that sucks mucus from your baby's nose.

Baby shampoo and soap

Baby carrier
For little ones, these carriers work great. We used ours in lieu of a stroller. They hold the child in front of you in a light, cloth sling. There are models that let you carry the child facing out as well as facing in. $20.

Snacks
You may not enjoy all the food you are offered. Consider bringing nutrition bars, beef jerky, trail mix, dried fruit and nuts.

Large book bag-type of purse
Bring something big enough to carry letter-size documents *all the time*. We used a carryall that did double duty as a briefcase/diaper bag. $20-30.

Money purse or money belt

Chances are you'll be carrying significantly large amounts of cash. Purchase a money belt designed to be worn underneath your clothing. (This is a safe precaution and a wise one. However, this is not to say that you should expect trouble. Law and order in China is hard, fast and rather Draconian. Crime is not the kind of problem it is here in the States. In time, we felt very comfortable walking the streets.)

Strollers

Don't bring a stroller. If you need one, buy it there for $15. That's where they're made.

Camera and/or camcorder gear and supplies

Dishwashing and detergent soap

... for in-room bottle and clothes washing. Backpackers use an all-purpose soap sold at REI and other camping retail stores.

Bactiguard

... for washing hands without a water source.

Baby clothes

Don't bring more than a half dozen changes. Better to buy in China after you know her size.

Medications for parents

Bring stuff for headaches, colds, flu, diarrhea, allergies.

Post-trip costs

$750 start-up costs plus $675 per month.

Day care: $440 per month
This is the big, ongoing expense. We have great day care for $440 a month that includes two meals each day. This is a terrific value. Day care can cost $1000 or more a month.

Clothing: $100
We spent maybe $100 max to get started. Stay away from the fancy labels! Forget frilly! Think functionality: Sweats, shoes and socks for cold weather and shorts and T-shirts for when it's warm. Buy new stuff as they grow. Chances are you'll be showered with things from friends and relatives anyway.

Food: $100 per month
Since Joy eats twice at day care, our food costs including formula aren't more than $100 each month.

Diapers: $60 per month
Seven diapers a day times 30 days equals over 200 diapers a month. A 68-pack of Huggies costs around $18 — you'll spend at least $60 each month on diapers.

Wipes: $25 per month
A mega pack of 68 wipes costs $5. If you use 10 each day you'll need 300 throughout the month. That's around $25 each month.

Furniture and gear: Around $500
When you know the age of your child, you will need

suitable furniture and gear, such as:

Bed (required after two years): $200.
Play pen: $40–100.
Chest of drawers with a changing table: $100–200.
Booster chair (straps onto an adult chair): $20–30.
Car seat (required by law): $60–100.
Stroller: $15 and up.

Summary of costs

Adoption:	**$17,294**
Supplies for trip:	**$250**
Post-trip:	**$750 to start,**
	$625 each month

You should have about $18,000 to spend initially and enough income to afford another $625 each month. This amount should put you in the hands of the very best adoption services. It should also enable you to comfortably provide (with good day care) for your new child.

Tax break for adoptive parents

From *Tax Benefits for Adoption*, Publication 968
(Rev. January 1998) Cat. No. 23402W
Department of the Treasury, Internal Revenue Service

Beginning in 1997, you may be able to take a tax credit of up to $5000 for qualifying expenses paid to adopt an eligible child. The credit can be as much as $6000 if the expenses are for the adoption of a child with special needs. The adoption credit is an amount that you subtract from your tax liability. After 2001, the adoption credit applies only to an adoption of a child with special needs and does not apply to an adoption of a foreign child.

Also, beginning in 1997, through 2001, up to $5000 ($6000) for a child with special needs) paid or reimbursed by your employer for qualifying adoption expenses under an adoption assistance program may be excludable from your gross income. An adoption assistance program for this purpose is a separate written plan set up by an employer to provide adoption assistance to its employees.

You may claim both a credit and an exclusion for expenses of adopting an eligible child. For example, for an eligible child who is not a child with special needs, you may be able to claim a credit of up to $5000 and also exclude up to $5000 from your income. However, you cannot claim both a credit and an exclusion for the same expense.

Full benefits are available for those who earn less than $75,000 in adjusted gross income the year they adopt. The credit disappears entirely at $115,000 of annual household income.

For further updated and in-depth information, send for Publication 968, *Tax Benefits for Adoption,* available through the Internal Revenue Service.

Joy in the Yang Dong Orphanage when she went by the name of Xiao Rou (Chinese for small and soft). She was approximately three days old when she was left on the front steps of the Civil Affairs Office in Yang Dong.

Chapter 3:

It Can Be Done!

Procedure and the paper trail
This is a long hike. It's not necessarily
difficult to perform but it may be
tedious. **It's important to be organized and patient.** Keep careful
records of each step. Missed details
can be stallers or stoppers just when
you thought you were finished.

From start to finish — from personal decision to
holding your baby — you should **expect a time line
of about one year.** For some, the length of the
process is hard because once you've made the big decision, *you want that child in your life now.* It helps to
consider that actually making your own baby takes
nine months.

It's wise to settle into and accept the paper trail and let
it run its course. Use the time to prepare yourself in
other ways for parenting a new child. This is especially
important for first-time parents. Time will go by faster
than you think.

About adoption procedure
There are three entities to deal with:
1. An **international child program**
2. A **homestudy adoption agency**
3. **Immigration and Naturalization Service (INS)**

Each have paperwork requirements. Taken all together the completion, compilation and submission of those requirements is a big, big job. But if approached with **patience** and a degree of **planning**, it's a chore that can be free of the epic frustrations that you may have heard about and fear.

Like Sandie Hicks, our gracious contact at Family Connections Adoptions, said to us, *It can be done!*

About the entities

It's no wonder that the paperwork requirements are daunting. **You are dealing with the governments of two countries and that of the state in which you live!**

An **international child program** is an agency approved by the Chinese government that finds your child (called the child referral), handles the adoption procedures in that country and arranges your travel and accommodations while you are there. They have working relationships with the Chinese government and their orphanages. They are your "Chinese Connection."

A **homestudy agency** is licensed in your state to fulfill the homestudy required by state law. A homestudy includes visits to the home, interviews and background checks on financial, health and criminal records. All foreign adoptions need a homestudy. This is a requirement of the international program and it's also a requirement of the INS. The homestudy agency provides the homestudy document as well as post-placement, which involves follow-up visits after the child arrives.

The **INS** is an agent of the United States federal government and they require that the child obtain a visa. They oversee the entire process to ensure that the child is coming here legally, that the family is aware of the process and that the family can take care of and be financially responsible for the child.

About these requirements

We decided <u>not</u> to list what each entity required at the time of our adoption for two reasons: (1) This stuff changes from time to time and prospective parents will be updated by their agencies when they decide to proceed with adoption. (2) Lists make very poor reading.

The point to make here about the paperwork requirements from each of the three agencies is that they overlap. Many of the documents have a common theme, or they are the same type of document on a different form. Thus, it requires an **overview** to best manage things. **Do not deal with these guys one at a time with blinders on.**

A plan

Nancy Cowie of Family Connections Adoptions likes to tell her clients to ***Put all three balls up in the air.*** That is, deal with your child program, your homestudy agency and INS all at the same time.

It is recommended that the family choose an international agency, or at least have a list of finalists that they can show to their homestudy agency. Then they need to request and obtain a list of all required documents from their international agency or agency finalists. **Your homestudy agency* can then review these lists of required documents along with their own list as well as that of the INS. With this information, they can help you set up a process to determine how many of each document is needed.** As a result, the proper number of specific documents can be obtained at one time without going back and doing it again.

For example, INS, your international agency and your homestudy agency all require proof of marriage, birth certificates and divorce decrees, if applicable. **If you have developed your total list of required documents from all three entities beforehand, you can send for the exact number of these documents you'll need.**

However, if you try to work with just one entity at a time you'll find yourself sending for the same materials again and again. Once you've hiked over the hill, it's frustrating and maddening to be told you need to do it again. Multiply that one hill several times and the process will seem endless and unendurable.

---

*In our case, the homestudy agency was near our home and our international child program was farther away. The homestudy document is also required by the other two agencies so you'll naturally begin with them. Furthermore, your homestudy agency may be more familiar with the processes of obtaining your domestic documentation than your child program. It should be noted that some agencies can function as both a homestudy agency and a child program, but that is not always true.

You've got to believe

Besides a plan you will need patience. It's a natural thing for prospective parents to want to wish away the red tape and all the time it takes to process your international adoption. But you cannot change time. It doesn't do any good to fret or get angry. So much of this is out of your hands and out of the hands of any single entity. Now is the time to develop the single most important thing after you've filled out the last form and laid out the last dollar: **Faith**.

More about agencies

Homestudy adoption agency
The first thing you do is choose your homestudy agency. Like choosing any contractor, look for references, study their services and fees and compare them with the competition. Talk to parents who have used them. Try to find one that is near you. **Look in the Resource Chapter** for a list of adoption organizations and state adoption agencies that may help you in your search.

Form after form after form ...
Your agency will take care of the homestudy reports required by law and help steer you through a river of required paperwork and legal procedures that include applications, fee agreements, fingerprint and child abuse clearances, certified copies of birth certificates, marriage certificates, divorce decrees, proof of health insurance coverage, work/salary verification, medical forms from your physician, release of school information (if applicable), self-studies, character references, visa petitions, re-adopt and finalization. These are spe-

cific things required in a specific way by specific bureaucrats in a specific order. Your agency should be able to guide you through what can be a convoluted experience.

Not to worry. Homestudies are OK
A homestudy involves visits to your home, interviews with each parent and various background checks on financial, health and criminal records. Re-adopt and finalization are legal procedures that parents take on when they come back from abroad with their children in order to obtain state birth certificates and adoption decrees.

Homestudies are not intrusive interrogations by men and women dressed in black suits and dark glasses. The licensed social workers that interview you aren't looking for perfect parents. **They want to make sure prospective parents are healthy,* emotionally stable, able to financially support the adoptive child and have not committed certain criminal acts.**

---

* It should be noted that our agency, Family Connections Adoptions, works with prospective parents who have a variety of health problems including those who must travel in wheelchairs, those who have had cancer, those with diabetes or cerebral palsy and even those who are blind. If their health problem is well managed and does not impair their ability to parent, they are welcome to adopt. For example, a diabetic will not be rejected if he regularly takes a physician's prescribed medication, gets checkups in a timely manner and diets and exercises properly. If the same person, however, did not take precautions and ignored medical advice, he would not be considered a suitable adoptive parent.

Your social worker is equally concerned about answering your questions about adoption and helping you prepare for life with the adopted child. Your agency will no doubt be made up of uniquely supportive and compassionate folks who care about the kids and you. They want you to succeed!

Our homestudy

We had an introductory or intake interview in the agency's office with a female social worker and three visits with interviews by the same friendly, male social worker in our home. He put together a report and we were approved. We received a copy of the report and by and large it was glowing, although he got some stuff wrong — like Kathleen's love of gardening (ha!) and my academic career (wrong college) — but what the heck. He saw the shining stars Kathleen and I can be and we passed the audition.

More importantly, the process helped us to understand and evaluate ourselves as people and prospective parents. Good homestudies make you dig deep — something every prospective parent, biological as well as adoptive, might find beneficial.

Subjects covered in our report

The six-page document covered a lot of ground. The report included:

Social worker's comments
Description of family members
Marriage and family interaction
Child rearing experiences and practices
Extended family

Financial situation
Home and neighborhood
Family health
Religion
Fingerprint and child abuse clearances
Summary of references
Motivation for adoption
Readiness for adoption
Acceptance of differences
Child desired
Evaluation and recommendation
Approval

During each interview he stressed that this was *not a test*. There was more or less an unspoken indication that we would be approved. The purpose of the homestudy was to give us a chance to gain some perspective about ourselves, our intentions and the journey we were about to take. They were casual, friendly and thoroughly enjoyable visits.

Immigration and Naturalization Service (INS)
The INS is very interested in your little import, of course. Your agency will send them stuff and you will send them stuff. Although you must deal with the INS directly at times, your agency will prepare you.

One of the trickier requirements is getting your visas. It helps to keep in mind that you're dealing with one of the more muscular bureaucracies around. If you follow directions and keep yourself organized, you'll be fine. Do not waste time arguing with government employees. They are right and you are wrong if they say you are wrong. Just do what they say!

The gentleman behind our international child program did not want us to mention his name or the name of his agency — but photos were OK. The success of our adoption was largely due to the extraordinary efforts of this fellow and his China Team.

International child program

Your international child program (approved by the Chinese government) will select your child and map out what is required to adopt the child in China. Much of the paperwork will be the same as before, perhaps with a twist or two. They will also arrange your itinerary, which includes flight plans, hotels, meals, trips to government offices and our own U.S. consulate. Pick your child program as carefully as you chose your homestudy agency. The latter will no doubt be able to supply a list of reliable services from which to choose.

You are in their hands

The idea here is to have an adoption and travel expert tell you when and how to make every move. **You are on a journey to meet your child, take her into the fold and come back home. You do not want to worry about food, beds, taxis or bureaucracies in a foreign country.** The international child program will tell you what to bring, when to show up at the airport and herd you to every place you need to go. They will hand you your child, stand over your shoulder when you fill out forms in government offices and explain why you are eating something that stares back at you.

Heritage

Adoptive parents must decide sooner or later how they want to address the heritage of their child. Obviously, if both parents are caucasian (like us) the little girl will realize in time that she is different. She is, in fact, Chinese and it's crucial that she feels comfortable with her ethnicity.

This can be a tricky subject. Although adoptive parents are bringing the child into their home and into a more affluent culture rich with opportunity, it may be unwise to label China or aspects of the Chinese culture in a negative manner. Parents may see themselves as saviors — saving a child from a rather meager existence and giving that child a better life. From there it's easy to develop a mind set that considers the Chinese way of thinking and doing things inferior.

Despite the arguments that may support such attitudes, the problem is that on some level the adopted child will take it personally because, again, she is Chinese. If parents think and say that China is a bad place then the child may think less of herself.

Our social workers sat us down in the beginning or our adoption procedure and tried to explain. *We don't want to whitewash these little girls* they said. *They must know who they are and where they come from. It's important to know and celebrate their Chinese roots.*

At first, I just nodded. I said nothing out loud during the meetings but I was *thinking* that as soon as our daughter's tiny feet hit California's Gold Coast she will know instinctively that she has become and will be for all time a California Girl — that state of being so desired by females of all persuasions the world over. Despite her Chinese heritage, she will naturally and eagerly embrace her California Girl-ness above all other considerations no matter what we do.

And as far as whitewashing, that would be impossible where we live — in a city situated close to the Mexican border with a hefty Hispanic population. I said *Heck, we live in a bona fide rainbow neighborhood. We've got Asian, African-American, Greek and Mexican-American neighbors. We even have a racially mixed marriage next door. It would take several coats of whitewash to cover all that!*

Which was and still is, quite true. But I still wasn't dealing with the issue of her being Chinese, our being white and the sort of situations that may develop in the world we inhabit. What are we going to do when folks want to know why an Asian child lives with us? What are we going to do when we confront bigotry? How do we tell her how to handle herself and her heritage in our neighborhood, our town, our region, our American culture?

After a year of having Joy, we aren't that much closer to

having answers to these questions. I guess we feel that our love for Joy and our honest answers to her questions will be enough. That and developing within her a powerful sense of self-worth. Kathleen and I will need to stand fast with our decision and be strong in our convictions, too. The world hasn't thrown us a curve yet, but it will happen.

These are sobering thoughts and the last thing prospective parents want to ponder when they're going through the adoption process. Folks in that position are eager to get to China and meet their daughters. But the fact remains that they are adopting a child from a different country and perhaps a different race. Sooner or later it's going to make a difference in their lives and hers. It's worth thinking about.

Chapter Four:
Preparing for a New Life

Practical preparations for having a new child in the family.

If you are as unfamiliar with babies as my wife and I were, you are in for a Titanic sea change.

The young child will become the center of your universe because you are IT to the baby. That kid depends on you and you alone for care, comfort and love. It's a stunning realization even after a year of research and red flag warnings from friends, parents, social workers and stand-up comedians.

You might think kids are like puppies or kittens. Look at all the care and patience your pets needed when they were young. You survived that OK, right? But within six months even the thickest dog can occupy itself and obey commands. Animals don't remain the helpless lumps that human rug crawlers are for most of the first year, or the heedless and fearless foragers that they become as toddlers.

The maturation process for human beings is very, very slow. You must think, prepare and plan for this child for years on end. It's a new life. The old one is gone.

Day care

In order to preserve your career you'll need to arrange for the care of your child when you work. This is absolutely crucial! Day care is not baby sitting. It's a whole lot more than that. The kid needs a second home with loving, reliable and experienced care. Find a good place before you come back with your baby.

Joy's day care: Grandmother Genie and Kathleen stop in to say hi. That's Norma Caro on the far right. Norma's in-home day care has become a cornerstone in our family's life.

You can get grandma, a nannie, a small neighborhood pre-school nursery or a larger operation that may even be franchised. Relatives are cheap but don't usually provide the stimulation that other children provide. Nannies are expensive and suffer the same problem, although they can give your child lots of individualized attention.

Smallish nurseries are inconsistent in terms of quality and services, but are often economical. Larger day care operations may provide a great deal but can be expensive and less attentive to individual kids.

We hired a next-door neighbor with a small child of her own to care for Joy for the first three months after we came back from China. It cost $1000 a month plus food, diapers and wipes. It was great for awhile, and then it wasn't. We didn't establish certain guidelines and one day our neighbor simply wasn't there. Not good. The casual give-and-take of friends, family and neighborly relationships may not work. Although people mean well, reliability can be an issue.

With a little research we finally found an ideal situation. In our neighborhood is a seasoned, professional in-home, licensed day care provider. The cost is $440 a month and includes two meals a day. This provider cares for about eight kids and has three caretakers in her employ.

The place is so good that parents usually keep their kids there until kindergarten. Norma Caro, the owner, is past president of the San Diego County Family Child Care Association. You cannot get better than that. We are thrilled with her loving and professional services and simply could not do without her.

Rituals

Think about how your days will play out. Especially mornings before work and evenings after you come home. The kid wakes, you diaper and dress, prepare breakfast for hungry people including yourself, supply large doses of attention and affection, get ready for the job, head out to day care and speed off to work. At night you pick up the kid, change, feed and entertain her as well as yourself, change and prepare the tot for sleepytime and finally convince your child it's time to knock off.

The better choreographed all this is, the better your lives will be. Kids need consistency. If you fly free-form your kid will fuss and you may never sleep soundly again.

Upheavals

Life with a new kid is not always like a greeting card. You are going to get sideswiped by some pretty heavy feelings. And you're going to feel pinched. This is especially true for the untested (first-time parents).

There is a need to anticipate and prepare for *resentment, anger, boredom and stress.*

Resentment because you've traded away your former carefree life.

Anger because until you can fully accept them for what they are, kids may seem to be trolls from hell.

Boredom because kids will take you away from what used to excite you. Caring for a child can be like watching the same 15-minute video over and over again.

Stress because you're changing your life forever — for good and not so good. You have more to think about, juggle and busy yourself with than ever before.

Goodbye leisure

Expect certain passions to wither. You won't have the time or freedom to pursue your old lifestyle unless you can afford a live-in nanny or your spouse desires to be a full-time, all-the-time mommy (fat chance). You should think about that. Learn that you will never be able to resume the same pattern and figure out what you can do to balance hobbies with baby.

Stuff to buy

Strollers

Get a cheap stroller for kicking around. For jogging or fast walking you'll need one of those three-wheeled jobs with a brake and inflatable tires.

Furniture

When you know the age of your child you can buy suitable furniture and equipment for sleeping (bed or crib), storage (closets and drawers), eating (booster or high chair) and traveling (car seats).

Clothing

Buy some basic items but get the rest *after* you come home. It makes little sense to buy much before you see the shape you're adopting. Despite the logic of this, you'll probably get all sorts of clothing from people who want to give you baby things. It's a kind and heartfelt ritual.

Food

Buy bottles and eating tools perhaps. The kid will have had a diet in the orphanage that you must wean him or her off of over time. Deal with that before you stock up on food.

Toys

We were delighted by a surprise shower of toys from friends and family. Toys you'll want to get, but kids don't need store-bought toys until they *think* they do. You'll have plenty of time for that.

Diapers

Throw-away, easy-to-strap-on-and-undo diapers come in packs of 68 for around $15. (How on earth did they do it before Huggies?)

Wipes

These specially designed, moistened towelettes for cleaning dirty bottoms also come in packs of 68 for $5.

Medicines

Buy baby medication for fever, cough, sneezing, congestion and pain.

Summary

Prepare first and foremost by taking the time to find good day care. If you don't think you need it, start imagining spending *all your time* with a young child. Better yet, find a friend with a kid and babysit (maybe all prospective parents should do this).

Next think about performing the day in and day out

stuff with a child. Think "Organized." If you're sloppy with housekeeping and schedules now, you'll be completely buried with a kid. Make space for the baby. Buy basic supplies, gear and furniture.

Think about all the feelings a new child in your life will bring. Anticipate joy and love, for sure. Anticipate gaining new maturity (even if you're middle-aged). Anticipate finding wonderful new places in your heart and head. But anticipate all the harsher (and equally valid) feelings, too.

Be ready, but hang loose. You'll figure it out!

Story: We have your baby!

The call from our agency was expected but it still surprised us.

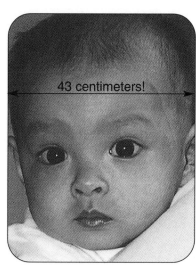

43 centimeters!

Hello, is this Doug Werner?

Yes.

This is Belle from your international child program. We have your baby!

Oh. Oh!

Do you have pen and paper? You might want to write this down.

Y-Yeah. OK.

Your baby's name is Yang Xiao Rou. Yang is her last name and indicates where she was born. Xiao Rou (pronounced He-ow Yo) means small and soft. She is ten months old.

Ten months! No kidding!

Yes. She is 65 centimeters long and weighs 6.5 kilograms. Her head is 43 centimeters and her chest is 44 centimeters.

Hold it! Her head is as big as her chest? What's wrong with her!

Babies have similar chest and head measurements. It's perfectly normal.

Really?

Yes.

Your group will be leaving for China in two weeks.

Two weeks!

Yes. Congratulations!

I still have the telephone notes I took that day. We were expecting a three-year-old because of our age. Getting an infant was unexpected and a little shocking. Kathleen was ecstatic when she heard the news.

Throughout the day I'd glance at the piece of paper with our daughter's specs scratched on it. Somewhere over 6,000 miles away someone had chosen a baby girl for us with a head 43 centimeters in circumference. And in just *two weeks* I'd be holding her in my arms.

Instant parents: Just two weeks after notification I was holding Joy in my arms.

Our Story

We enjoyed China very much. The people were surprisingly warm, kind and cheerful. All the Chinese we met were happy for Joy (calling her Lucky One) and for us, too. This impressed me very, very deeply.

As an American raised during the Cold War, I did not expect open arms. I thought the officials involved with the adoption would be civil, but I certainly didn't think everyday people would care for us much. It was stunning to witness their pleasant nature and the well wishes we received strolling the city streets with Joy.

On the bus back from Yang Dong the day after we got her. Joy is ten months old.

In the journal I talk about that and a lot of other things including the food I didn't care for, dirty air and filthy rivers. No, the trip and the China we saw weren't perfect, but I am certainly not trying to discredit the country or our agency. We are telling the truth so that prospective parents might have a better idea of what to expect when they arrive. You know, you can't go to Disneyland without battling freeways and standing in line.

Keep this in mind: This is our take on the trip. Others in the group had similar experiences, of course, but they also had different ones. For example, many thought the food was fine. Some parents say it's the best Chinese food they ever had. Go figure. Maybe I'm just finicky. Maybe they're nuts.

But seriously, here's the most important thing: We encourage people to take the trip and to adopt Chinese children. There are so many wonderful babies over there who need a home. It's a marvelous and worthy decision to make for yourselves.

Doug and Kathleen Werner

Chapter Five:
Being
There

*A journal of our
trip to China.*

8-16-98

The day has finally arrived. We
make final preparations and
hit the road for Los Angeles
International Airport (LAX) around 3:30 p.m. We stop at
Tamarack Beach so I can surf before we fly. We continue to San Clemente and stop at a Coco's for dinner
at 6. (Little did we know that it would be the best meal
we'd eat for almost two weeks.) We leave for LAX and
after getting lost trying to find the long-term parking
lot, we park, disengage the van battery, drag seven
pieces of luggage on and off a shuttle, wait in line for
90 minutes to check our bags and finally settle next to
our gate. It's now 11, and since we're both early birds,
we start to tire.

The most interesting thing about the trip so far is
watching Kathleen pull her passport from her money
belt that has become tangled in her bra. The guy at the
check-in counter takes this in stride. In line with us is a
crowd of perhaps 100 Chinese kids dressed in cowboy
hats and Mickey Mouse ears. Is this some kind of
omen?

At the gate waiting for the early morning flight, we're

The sweltering weather will define our journey.

dingy, excited and a little nervous — but mostly glad. Folks from our groups gather and we watch two young Chinese girls dance and play. We learn that they were adopted from China and that their parents are going back for a second child. Kathleen and I consider that a good sign.

The flight is sixteen hours. We get some sleep. Unremarkable food. Pretty Chinese attendants. Not so bad overall. At one point I wander to the back of the plane and ask a group of attendants resting there if we will land in the morning or evening. Since we're traveling halfway across the globe, I'm confused about time. I thought it a simple question, but they just sit in a row looking at me with wondering faces. Later Kathleen asks for aspirin. An attendant makes three trips, first bringing a spoon, then salt, then soup. Finally Kathleen makes a face and points to her head and the attendant exclaims *Oh! Ass-per-eeeen!*

8-18-98 (Gaining a day)
It's daybreak when we reach China. Flying in, the view of mountains peaking through a mist reminds us of traditional Chinese landscape prints — snaking rivers, unusually shaped peaks and clouds. As the plane taxies, I see trees running along the ridges that surround the airport. An unusual and beautiful sight. Looks like China.

Getting off the plane on wobbly legs, the weather wraps around us like a hot, wet blanket. (The swel-

tering weather will define our journey. That and the
ice-cold buses and hotel rooms.) We stick to Norman,*
our group leader, like glue. The airport is sparse and
clean. Lots of tile.

Many young men in military uniform. Some sullen
looking. When I try to take photos in the airport, one
of them stops me
quite abruptly
with a sharp
shout. This is
startling and to
any American,
insulting. Wisely,
I let it go with-
out a peep. (It's
actually the only
rude moment
I'll have on the
trip.) We wade
through more of

Guangzhou is a very busy, bustling place.

these serious looking guards, dressed in the classic Red
Chinese style you see in the movies and file into a
waiting bus outside the terminal.

The bus trip through the city is phantasmagoric. We're
all spacey from the flight and here we are on a major
thoroughfare replete with bicycles, motor scooters, the
smallest cars I've ever seen and streams of people on
their feet. Strapped to the back of many scooters are
cages of chickens and ducks. It's a teeming, streaming
scene and nobody bothers to stay in a lane, brake or
even look around them as they peddle, motor or hoof
to somewhere in a big hurry. Someone in our group

Don't sleep! You in China!

quips *They wasted the paint used for lanes!* Guangzhou (formerly Canton) is a city of eight million and I think they're all out today. Kathleen calls the town an exotic and very large Tijuana.

Meanwhile, Norman stands in front of the bus with a microphone and rattles on about various things in his clipped, wry, almost unintelligible manner. I catch him saying something about *No discussion with other groups because jealousy,* which means he does not want us to discuss our itinerary with his competition. He also says *All of us aunties and uncles to all children,* meaning we all have to care for each other and each others' kids on the trip. He finally says *Don't sleep, you in China!* because although many of us are tired from the flight, our stay is short and we should stay awake and soak up what we can.

The China Hotel has a Hard Rock Cafe and looms next door to a big McDonald's. The hotel is surprisingly opulent with uniformed help opening doors and ushering us across the vast, icy cold lobby. There are 57 people total in our group (made up of two groups). We gather in a meeting room to get information and room keys. With little fuss, we get keys and find our rooms on the twelfth floor overlooking a tenement. It's a nice room. Five-star all the way. Kind of unsettling to see the poverty right there, only a few yards away, though.

I'm eager to hit the streets to see the *real* China before lunch. Bicycles, taxis, motorbikes, fumes, streaming people, heat, humidity, lavish billboards in Chinese and staring faces all add up to a unique and exciting situation. I dig it. Kathleen does not. We walk a block in the smothering heat and smog when Kathleen becomes uncomfortable about hiking with a loaded money belt (neither of us have ever carried so much cash — we would have been nervous anywhere!). On the way back, an old beggar woman wants a handout. We give her some change and she gives us a toothless smile and a thumbs up. She will be one of the very few beggars we come across. Although few are affluent, the people we see on the street are neat in appearance, either busy making a living or going somewhere in a hurry.

Later, we head out on buses for lunch at what our itinerary says is a "fancy" restaurant. On the way we meet Martin, one of the China Team members and the designated "tour guide" for the trip. He stands in the front of the bus with a microphone and says

Voice of Martin! About adopted kids: "Born wrong stomach, find right door!"

Now listena to Voice of Martin. His English is just as tangled and endearing as Norman's. We get a short history lesson on the bus ... *China opened in 1979 ... tallest building in Guangzhou 88 story ... China suffering worst floods in 300 years ... crime not a problem because punishment is harsh ... hot weather makes for siesta time in afternoon ...*

We travel on a bridge across a river and it's the most

People live on top of each other (I think of bee hives).

polluted water I've ever seen. Almost black with filth. Someone shouts *Let's go swimming!* We pass lots of buildings with lion statues guarding the doors. There's construction everywhere and all the buildings being worked on are covered with webs of bamboo scaffolding. The bamboo poles are like tree trunks. Really thick and wide and long.

My general impressions of the city so far (in my dazed, uprooted state) are that it's made up of projects (like, say, in Detroit or Queens) where people live on top of each other (I think of bee hives). It's dirty. The atmosphere is gray-green with no sun peaking through the awful smog. There are colorful, even beautiful billboards everywhere and all around, of course, you see Chinese lettering — so elegant and graceful. Probably advertising soda pop, but all I understand and appreciate is the graphic splendor.

Lunch is not bad. Big round tables each with a giant Lazy Susan that servers keep loaded with dim sum. This is a collection of eatables that in no way reminds me of Chinese food back home. (This will be the last Chinese meal I actively partake as my taste for the authentic wilts fast.) Nice restaurant though. Very classy, in stark contrast to the streets.

After lunch we go shopping at the Friendship Mall. Inside it's all shiny and chock-full of merchandise in countless displays on several floors. Pretty salesgirls everywhere. We look at ivory trinkets and sculptures and jade jewelry. Kathleen buys jade chopsticks from enthusiastic employees. After a bit we start to tire. It's been a long, long day ...

We bus back to the hotel. Back in the room, Kathleen naps. I read and fall asleep, too.

Bamboo scaffolding and construction everywhere!

It's difficult to wake for dinner. We watch some kind of military youth channel on television. I can't understand much, but I gather the message is *Everything and everybody for the State*! Young men and women wear olive-green uniforms (with no undershirts), red shoulder bars, black-brimmed hats and open collars. I see a contrast between the helter-skelter of street life with the regimentation of army life (or whatever this is). They even clap hands at the same time after somebody's speech. This seems really odd. Television here portrays bold primary colors (Red! Green! Yellow!)

We gather in the lobby at the appointed hour and troop next door to another restaurant. I cannot eat the food. I have a difficult time even *looking* at it since the head is left on one of the chicken dishes. Lunch was better and that's not saying much. But there's entertainment! — a variety act like we used to see on the old Ed Sullivan Show. It's a family of plate twirlers, contortionists and gymnasts that includes three boys, two men,

Everybody is selling something. It's a city of peddlers.

and three voluptuous, big-hipped women. They are very, very good. But we're too weary to stay long. We leave early, find our way back to the hotel and by 8:30 we're in bed.

Wednesday 8-19

I'm up at 6 a.m. I run in the hotel's small courtyard, up the stairs and around the roof. It's so hot already! I'm almost faint from the effort. A young girl is wailing in the courtyard garden with a friend sitting by. It's eerie and sad.

Breakfast buffet is not bad. Iffy eggs, good service. Lots of things to eat. (The buffet will provide the only meals I heartily eat in China.)

We take the cool, cool bus to the adoption agency. Our papers include a photo of Joy. It's our first look. (Although photos of Joy were available long before the trip, we opted not to see them since we were told that doing so might create expectations). Kathleen bonds and cries. Just to be ornery, I say *I don't know ... she looks shifty-eyed to me.* Kathleen laughs and cries some more.

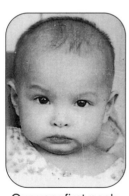

Our very first peek.

She *does* have very *round* eyes and a *big* bald head. She also has a rather serious look (where's that happy-to-meet-you smile?) Not

quite the image we
expected (black hair, bowl
haircut and slits for eyes),
but it's just a passport
photo.

The interview and signing
is short and easy. The
Chinese agent is very
friendly. Lots of clapping
and good cheer. They ask
us if we have seen the
photo and if we accept
her. They want to know
our plans for her and if
we promise not to

No slackers in this town.

abandon her. Norman stands close by and monitors the
whole thing.

I take photos of the office scene jammed with parents.
We go outside where a local TV crew is filming our
group. There are interviews with parents and members
of the China Team. We make a donation to the victims
of the recent flooding.

Lunch is in a restaurant on a polluted lake on the west
side of the city. It's the same food as last night. Greasy
and glistening with Ghostbuster's Slime (somebody
says it's corn starch). Again, chicken is served with the
head. The smells outside the restaurant are nauseating!
My appetite is utterly destroyed. (This smell pops up
everywhere throughout the trip. I think it's the water.)

Our ride through town is fascinating. Rows of small

We are soon to become parents. *Instant* parents.

shops in old buildings. Everybody is selling something. It's a city of peddlers. More of that projects look. I note that many of the buildings have a tile exterior. Like the tiles in a shower. So odd and amusing to see a 12-story building coated with small shower tiles.

Bus trip to Yang Dong

We load up and leave the city in the afternoon, bound for the town of Yang Dong (no kidding) where Joy's orphanage is located. There's some open country, a few belching factories and lots of boxy buildings. We cross more dirty rivers and see lots of junks.

We pass farms made up of small rectangles of crops. The gray, smoggy sky begins to clear as we travel away from the city. There are miles of uninteresting, run-down buildings. Then here and there rises a palatial building in contrast.

Martin wants to have *Group Experience!* and starts talking in the microphone. Clipped but informative, he says *In China, dogs for food, birds for pets* when we pass a huge bird market. When we pass a giant factory spewing smoke he says *Cremation plants. Must hold breath.* About Chinese adopted children he says *Born in wrong stomach, found right door.* He wants us to ask him questions and have an open dialogue, but we're bushed. Many nod off. He gives up.

After a while we stop because the other bus in our entourage gets a flat. Everyone takes the stop in good humor and Norman passes around cool bottles of water and soda.

The tire is fixed and we head out. Seeing that we're a little more awake, Martin tries to engage us again. *There are 10,000 Chinese babies adopted each year ... 4,000 go USA ... Modern state founded 1949 ... Mao ... help from USSR ... Our big brother ... In 1958 China and USSR relationship ends ... from 1966 to 1976 is Cultural Revolution ...*

Fixing a flat on the road to Yang Dong. No big deal. We laughed it off.

We make a rest stop in a dusty town. The facilities are pretty bad. No toilets, just basins on the floor to squat over. Martin tells me that the Chinese think it's more hygienic. We buy pop and snacks at a nearby hotel. Martin buys a few bags of what look like grapes with a very thick, tough skin. You eat the insides and spit out the hide.

The long ride ends at dusk. Our hotel rises majestically out of the local squalor. Again, accommodations are opulent and ice-cold from the air conditioning. Our rooms come with a tiny bed for the baby and a complimentary rattle. It hits us that we are soon to become parents. *Instant* parents. This is beginning to feel momentous.

You get child today!

Dinner is in the hotel at 7 p.m. Same Lazy Susan setup, same dim sum grub. I sit next to an interesting lady who is a casting director from Los Angeles. She's adopting a child as a single mother and has her sister with her. Both have a great sense of humor and we share a few laughs about the thornier aspects of our journey. Back in our room I eat one of the ten Cliff Bars I packed.

Waiting for Joy.

Thursday 8-20

The day has finally arrived. Up at 5:45 a.m., Kathleen walks and I jog. It's very hot and humid. I run for 30 minutes. The surrounding area has lots of construction. I pass shanties and some older folks doing tai chi. Breakfast is another round of dim sum. I eat another Cliff Bar. After the meal Norman says *Go back room, wait for phone call and baby. You get child today!* In a very short while, Lucy, one of the China Team members, knocks on our door. Here we go!

We meet on the seventh floor, in front of the elevators. Apparently the children are waiting in another room with caretakers just around the corner from where we stand. Anticipation is thick. Excited parents-to-be either pace or stand trembling with excitement. Norman, the master of ceremony, gathers us together and gives a short speech with a big buildup before we meet our children. Before he finishes, one of the caretakers gets her signals crossed and comes around the corner with the first child. He actually sends her back saying *I not ready yet!* — this in front of the expectant Mom who is wide-eyed and quivering as she sees her little one

Mom gets her first.

approach only to be taken back. This is either grand theater or torture, but Norman's final statement is brief and the babies are finally brought out one by one.

Hi Daddy!

As each parent's name is announced, a caretaker comes round the corner with a child and places her in the mother's arms. This is beyond words. Probably the most emotionally charged moment of all our lives. There's not a dry eye in the house. We are about the third called. Little Joy is quiet yet alert as she is placed in Kathleen's arms. *She's a keeper* I say. After a moment Kathleen gives her to me and I realize that I haven't held a baby in years. Now I'm holding *my daughter.*

Who designs baby clothing anyway? Dr. No?

When all adoptive parents have their baby, we pile into a nearby room to learn about formula. A roomful of babies and not a peep as the girls from China Team show us how to prepare the thick formula (rice cereal and milk) that the kids are used to. So thick (like pancake batter) you need to lop off the tip of the nipple with a pair of scissors.

Back in our room, we make formula and feed our little girl for the first time. Later, we are called back down to complete some paperwork for the local Chinese officials. Team members Sarah, Grace and Lucy translate and it goes smoothly.

That afternoon we change diapers for the first time. I take one side and Kathleen the other. It's comical but we get it done. She does not like to be on her back for her diaper change. Then we wrestle her into jammies and try to stuff her into the Snuggly Carrier. There's much crying. But a walk around the hallways calms her down.

Dressing Joy is difficult. It feels like we're tearing her tiny limbs off putting her into the jammies. Who designs baby clothing anyway, Dr. No? The Snuggly is beyond us. Too many straps and adjustments. We go to lunch. Joy is very quiet and subdued throughout. Other babies are up and active. Kathleen is worried, thinking Joy is slow or something. Smiling Sarah comes by and says all is well.

Back in the room we play with her and get her to smile for the first time by tickling her chin. Kathleen and I make fun of her frowny face, lumpy cheeks, thick eyebrows and wispy sideburns. She falls asleep for about 30 minutes. Changing diapers and dressing her for the second time is easier. She cries, but gets over it quickly.

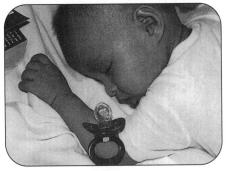

She sleeps a lot. Four naps a day.

We discuss whether Joy is cute or not. I think her eyebrows are too big, chin too weak, head too lumpy. Kathleen says she's cute. Sarah says she's cute. Everyone else says she's cute. Nice eyes for sure. She enjoys playing with an aspirin bottle and the rattler that came with the room.

Later on, after working out in the hotel gym, I cross the lobby where the hotel manager approaches me. I'm soaking wet and I think that he's about to chastise me for being such a slob in his sparkling hotel. He's a young Chinese dude, maybe 25, and dressed like Cary Grant. He smiles and says *Please sir, if I can assist you in any way at all let me know!* Well, what do you know. Relieved, I give him a thumbs up and a big thanks.

Thursday evening
We take a walk outside. Someone sees a snake. There's a fly or two but surprisingly (because we seem to be in a lush, delta region) no bugs. Joy's awake and doing

> **She's only happy if she's held and walked. I walk and walk and walk.**

fine. Locals parade in front of the hotel. Young girls wear tight cutoffs and stylish shades.

Our meal has an American wrinkle tonight (our hosts clearly want to please us). It includes a plate of fried eggs and a small plate of french fries. Everyone has babies now. The dining room is full of them. One couple in our group, Randy and Toni, have a 15-month-old with very big, expressive eyes. She's quiet and cute with graceful hands and long legs. Toni is not tall and the kid is large on her lap. They are very happy.

During dinner Joy sleeps, but wakes and moans. Sarah checks her out and brings over a doctor, a pretty young women, who says Joy has a fever. Kathleen takes her upstairs for some medication, I go up soon thereafter.

Later Sarah and the doctor show up at our room and give Joy a shot and insert a pill up her butt. Joy is very unhappy about that. Only a long, long walk through the halls settles her down. Finally around 9:30 she conks out and she sleeps all night.

Friday 8-21
We wake her at 5 a.m., change her diapers (still no dump) and make formula, although she wants to play first. She's particularly fascinated with our shiny, foil-stamped paperback books. Soon she goes for the bottle. Then she chows down another. Joy's a new girl today. Very happy, smiling, alert and energetic. She plays

with the aspirin bottle and rattler, rocks on her stomach and gets up on hands and knees. She's happy to lie on the bed and play, doesn't need to be picked up and doesn't cry (only a frown or two). Nothing like yesterday. She falls asleep around 6:45 a.m.

I run to a distant dam and back in about 30 minutes and miss a group breakfast of hot dogs and spaghetti (*that* must have been a treat). I jog past a crew of coolies tiling the top of the dam (I'm told tiling is a cheap way to prepare exteriors, but I'm thinking they just like tile). Along the way is a loud, honking goose farm. Rice patties are everywhere. In the far distance I see more of the monolithic buildings the Chinese like to create. Impressive from a distance but empty, cheap and institutional up close.

The view from our room.

After the jog, I wash in our room and head down to the restaurant. Back in the room Joy plays by herself on the floor. She crawls and tries to stand. Lots of rocking. She chews on her colorful paperback book. Not interested in formula yet. Kathleen and the baby nap. I try to do some laundry in the bathroom sink with limited success. I hang shirts to dry in our picture window overlooking the lake. The view from here is impressive. The delta stretches green toward a

But it's my *duty!*

large skyline that we couldn't see when we first arrived.

Joy wakes up crying and fusses for a few hours. She's only happy if she's held and walked. She still won't take a bottle. She has a very runny nose and hates to have it wiped. She also has wet diapers and hates to be changed. I pick her up and we walk and walk and walk. During lunch she does OK for a while, but she's always on the verge of tears. This is our introduction to some of the challenges of having a baby. It's difficult when we can't find the source of her discontent. At 1:30 p.m. she finally falls asleep.

This journal is about adoption, Joy, China, us in China and could easily become a Joy book. She's so precious when comfortable and happy. Hopefully, yesterday was an aberration — a combination of shock, unease and fever.

I nag Kathleen about organizing baby stuff to make it easier for feeding and diaper changes. I'm right, up to a point, but probably a little Prussian. I'm the one telling her to wipe Joy's mouth and change her clothing, but it's Kathleen who makes the formula, packs and oversees everything.

With Sarah, one of the China Team members. Our friend and devoted guide.

Joy sleeps like she's dead.

Friday afternoon

Sarah stops by. We thank her for the help last night. She seems surprised that we'd say such a thing and says *But it's my duty!* This knocks us out. How admirable. So gratifying to think someone with this attitude is on our side during this journey.

We visit with Joy's former caretaker who has come to the hotel from the orphanage to meet with the government people officiating the adoption. A kindly woman who knows Joy by sight, she takes Joy and the baby smiles at first, then cries. This is Joy's MO today, but it also may mean she's beginning to bond with us. We're encouraged to discover that Joy had people in the orphanage who knew

Coolies, water buffalo and rice patties outside of Yang Dong. Just like years ago.

and cared for her. So often you fear that the children are neglected or worse.

It rains this afternoon and it's gusty for a short while. The buses back to Guangzhou don't leave until 4:30. Kathleen and I spend the time walking Joy for miles in and around the freezing lobby.

We finally board and it's nice to be headed back to Guangzhou. It's slow going at first. We stop and take photos outside Joy's orphanage, but we cannot go inside. The building is plain and has no air condi-

Small children, older folks, everybody smiles and says *Hi!*

tioning. It's not really dismal, but almost. During a rest stop we buy peanuts. We drink bottled water and lukewarm soft drinks (nothing is really cold in China except the air conditioning). We travel through the delta and see farmers wading through rice paddies with their water buffalo. It's like looking at an old Chinese print come to life. Now and then we pass what look to be ancient castles. From the comfort of the bus, it looks pastoral, but in truth it must be a hot and humble life out there.

The last leg of the trip is trying. Too long with a squirmy kid. A combination of boredom, bumpy roads, wild driving (these guys drive like NASCAR drivers, somehow no one gets hit or run over), smog, heat and humidity.

Getting back to the China Hotel is wonderful. In the lobby members of the local orchestra, dressed to the nines, play various tunes including the theme from "Titanic." Although we've seen the movie and heard the song more than a few times, we are deeply moved by it in this context. Probably because the arrangement and the musicianship are so good. That syrupy song sounds so fine and fitting to our journey. It could be the theme song for our trip.

I head for the McDonald's next door. With the help of a translator, I order a Big Mac and fries. I wouldn't touch this stuff back in the states, but after a few dim sum dinners, it tastes great. Kathleen is ready for the sack by

9 p.m. Joy is a wonder. She smiles as we change her and prep for bed. She rocks herself in the crib. Content and happy, she emits an array of babbling, growling, snorting and moaning sounds. By 10:30 we're asleep. Joy wakes at 12:30 and 3:30 a.m. I change wet diapers, walk her around the room and feed her some formula, which she wolfs down. Kathleen's back is causing her a problem and she has trouble doing some of these things. I take over and it's OK, once I get out of bed.

Saturday 8-22
She's awake by 6 a.m. Kathleen and she take a bath together — something Kathleen has been looking forward to. Afterward, we play with her on the carpet.

Yeah, this looks like China. The hotel next to ours had this pretty garden.

We go down for breakfast at 7. Joy is asleep. Breakfast is great. Good coffee, ham, bacon, waffles and fruit. All you can eat. I have trouble eating with her in my arms. Kathleen puts her in the Snuggly. It's best to trade her off and eat in shifts.

After that we go next door to shop in what is called the Times Square Mall. We look for a stroller but have no luck. Lots of good art, though. Classic Chinese styles as well as Western spinoffs. There are van Gogh look-alikes as well as photo realistic and impressionistic

Bay-bee! Bay-bee!

styles. We like what we think are the authentic/traditional Chinese-styles best.

A nearby courtyard is beautiful. There are gardens of small sculpted trees, Buddha carvings, a lily pond and pagodas. It strikes us that, at last, we're in a setting that looks like the China in our minds. A little boy comes up to me and says *Hello, how are you?* I say *Hello, how are you?* He says *Fine.* I ask *Do you speak English?* No reply. I try something else, but he's at the end of his education and runs away.

Joy passes out. We stroll through another maze of shops and stores. They sell everything but strollers. We are the center of attention with the baby. Small children, older folks, everybody smiles and says *Hi!* An older lady shows Kathleen how to support Joy's head as she leans out of the carrier. This unsolicited help from people on the street is common throughout the trip. The excursion is fun and real to me. Like I'm finally getting a taste of China.

Joy seems heavier as her sleep deepens. We go back to the hotel at 10:30 a.m. We call Kathleen's parents, Gene and Genie. They sound like they're next door. They are very interested in our trip. Gene calls himself *Zumi* (Chinese for grandfather).

The ever-friendly maids come in to change the sheets and exclaim *Bay-bee! Bay-bee!* when they see Joy. They want to hold her. Joy is wide-eyed from the attention then starts crying. Stimulus overload!

This little girl. So much has changed in her life. From a crib among many, loved and cared for up to a point — now showered with new faces, hands, places and sounds. The epicenter of our lives forever.

Nice room until we came. Joy sacks out on the rug.

We have a different room and view from the one we first checked into. The street below is teeming with traffic. At one point I count 25 taxis headed around the bend at the same time. There are rows and rows of parked motorbikes. The interaction of vehicles and pedestrians is like watching ants on parade. Or like blood cells streaming through intersecting capillaries. There seems to be a magic sensor surrounding each moving thing, preventing accidents. It looks unbelievably chaotic, but there are never any mishaps. Tiny motorbikes zoom between careening buses. People stroll across the highway unconcerned and unharmed by speeding drivers.

There are buildings as far as I can see. Half the city seems to be under construction. Lots of green trees and hills. There's an interesting old gymnasium across the street, but most buildings I see are monolithic blocks of mirrored glass, cement and tile. A huge "Mita" billboard is directly across from our window and shines in on us at night.

The park is a reflection of the China I imagined. Cultural splendor and majesty.

I stand at the window with Joy. She's naked on the sill, little hands pressed against the glass, looking down at the hustle-bustle. What does she see?

I will try to get down there with my camera this afternoon and record some images. Up to this point it has been a tightly scheduled existence. But now we've got six days to loosen up.

Kathleen goes to the hotel gym while Joy sleeps and I wash a bunch of my things in the bathtub using detergent and shampoo. Kathleen comes through the door as Joy awakens. We have some trouble changing and feeding. Lots of crying. There's some tension between Kathleen and me. We decide to organize the baby procedures.

The park is loaded with sculpture as well as exotic plants, trees and flowers.

We go out for lunch without the group which means we must pay for it. Joy starts to cry at the table. I gladly leave with her (why eat in an expensive restaurant anyway?). We play for 10 minutes, I walk her until she falls asleep and then put her to bed. Kathleen comes back disappointed in her meal and its price tag.

Enjoying his patch of serenity. China Hotel is just across the street.

Saturday afternoon

I go for a walk. No destination. My goal: photos of street life. I end up in a park that runs alongside the China Hotel. I pay two yuan (60 cents) to get in. There are waterways with paddle boats and fountains. Gardens everywhere. Shady walkways. It's very pretty and a sharp contrast to the street. Serene. There's music coming from speakers and it's strange and soothing. A sculpture garden is a grand surprise. There are a number of different themes and styles — all quite good. The park is a reflection of the China I imagined. Cultural splendor and majesty.

The air changes. All at once there's thunder, lightning and showers. I'm unprepared, without even a camera case. I run under some trees, but it's very leaky there. I head for a roof I see in the distance. I run down slippery, tiled stairs. The roof belongs to a toy car ride. There are a lot of people under it. I'm the only foreigner. Folks are friendly. They say *Hello!* I say *Hello! How are you!* The storm rages for several minutes. It cools the superheated air. A nice bit of weather. The lightning cracks again and it reminds me of summer thunderstorms back home, only more powerful.

As it subsides, I try to seek an exit, but I'm lost (it's a big, big park). I ask directions from an attendant who's

> **Everybody has a mobile phone here — everybody.**

very happy to point the way. I come upon the Sun Yat-sen Memorial, an obelisk on top of a hill (sort of like San Francisco's Coit Tower). I climb the stairs to the top. From there the city looks enormous. The skyline is dramatically larger than I expected and stretches forever. It's so vast that I think of comic book renderings of megalopolises of the future.

I find the street by myself, but soon I'm lost again. I wander. Small shops sell firecrackers, shiny party and parade things and people, people, people are everywhere. A one-legged beggar follows me for a block until I give him 10 yuan. He's very grateful. In the overcast, dampness and gray this scene is soaked with character. Like something out of an old sailor's story.

I ask *Where China Hotel?* to passersby and they point me in the right direction. A man strolling with his wife and child actually stops me and asks if he can help (I guess my predicament is that obvious).

Later, a young man on a motorbike stops to assist. He's very inquisitive and armed with an English dictionary. He wants to know where I'm from, where I'm staying — all this on a crowded sidewalk. I'm impressed but wary. And anxious to return to our room. He wants to show us around on Monday, his day off. He gives me his pager number (everybody has a mobile phone here — *everybody*), wants our hotel room number and our name. I decline and feel a little bad about it, but I'm unwilling to commit. I finally shake the guy, look across the street and there's the China Hotel. I'm glad to get back in the room and to relax in the cool, cool air.

Kathleen and Joy look refreshed from naps. We go to the market next door for water and soft drinks (we choose from Coca-Cola, Sunkist Orange and Sprite). Joy is happy to travel and loves the sights and activity. She sort of purrs sometimes. It sounds like a contented growling. She falls asleep in the room when we get

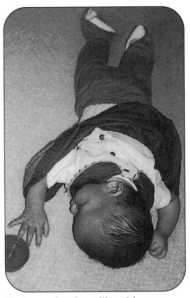

If she only slept like this now. Note her ensemble. Mom and Dad's first efforts to dress Joy are pretty sad.

back. We take her that way to a pizza party in Norman's room. It's a very festive affair. Babies and parents pile in. Joy wakes eventually and enjoys the party.

I take some photos. The Round Table Pizza tastes great! I stuff myself. Kathleen wears a red-hot outfit. Joy has her Green Hornet jammies on and together they look like Christmas. It's also one of the parent's birthday. There's a cake and a card signed by all. We leave around 7:30 p.m.

Joy stays awake. I play with her for some time. Kathleen is put out — she is tired and wants to go to bed. I want her to play with the kid, too. She just wants to feed Joy and be done with it. She makes formula,

> People are charming and friendly. A lady in the park laughs and tells me Joy's outfit is too warm. I let her hold the baby.

burning her hand in the process, yet Joy doesn't want it. Oh boy. Kathleen is frustrated. I say *Better get used to it!* She ponders that (then *I* ponder that) It's awesomely true.

We put an awake girl to bed expecting the worst. But she rocks herself to sleep with tiny grunts and other unique noises. It's a miracle. Thank you, Lord!

Sunday 8-23
She sleeps all the way through the night. Some kicking around but no wide-awake crying. Kathleen changes her and Lo! a dump at last! Hard, brown, little rabbit pellets. Still no crying. We feed her one bottle and go to breakfast. Toward the end of the meal she's grumpy. In the room she fusses on the floor and passes out. What a dame. Kathleen goes to the gym.

This journal has become a Joy book with a China subplot. This girl has taken over our world.

The groups are rounded up in our two buses to go shopping. This time we go to a store that sells mostly jade. There we meet an artist who spells out your baby's name in Chinese on a long scroll. This is a poetic, traditional thing. The result is wonderful — a heartfelt, genuine, personal piece of art. We also buy two Chinese landscapes by the same artist. This gen-

tleman is a very generous soul. We are very pleased
with the purchases.

We go to a Buddhist temple to get our new children
blessed. This is very moving and an authentic experience. Three huge bronze Buddhas, with monks,
incense, banyan trees, the works. The weather is hot,
hot, hot. A local woman gestures to Kathleen to undress
Joy who is wearing her
full length jammies. We
strip the baby to the
waist. Even so she's soon
covered with sweat, but
she's very good
throughout the morning.
Kathleen carries her all
day.

Lettering Joy's very own scroll.

Afterward, we go to lunch
at the same place we
went on our second day,
where I nearly fainted
from the smell. I decide
not to eat and instead
take Joy around the lake.
We stroll past a number
of tiny shops to a park. Real street life. People are
charming and friendly. A lady in the park laughs and
tells me Joy's outfit is too warm. I let her hold the baby,
but Joy doesn't like it. The baby is happy with the walk
until we get back to the restaurant. While we wait outside, she gets fussy. She does not like to sit still!

Back at the hotel, Kathleen bathes Joy. I go to the gym

Monica? Missiles in India? Sorry, but we're a little busy right now making our own history!

and work out for an hour. It's a very nice facility. Nothing like the closet in Yang Dong. First-class equipment. Mirrors, music and thick carpet. Overlooking the pool and skyline.

All three of us go next door to the market to get food, drink and clothing for the baby. A fellow with our group generously lends me 200 yuan as I'm very low on Chinese cash. The market doesn't take American dollars. The same guy later comes by the room with some homemade beef jerky that he prepared for the trip. It tastes marvelous!

We hustle downstairs to eat with the group in one of the hotel restaurants. Joy goes nuts. I'm tired and impatient. Seats are hard and uncomfortable. Service sucks and I finally blow. Kathleen comforts the kid and we finish our meal. I feel sheepish about my outburst because this is obviously such a kind-spirited, kid-loving bunch. My hot head is out of place. But I don't think anyone really minded. I imagine most of

The Snuggly Carrier is an indispensable part of traveling.

Has capitalism taken root? They call this shopping center Times Square Mall.

them probably understood.

Back in the room, Joy is prepped for bed and bedded. She only cries half-heartedly. I think we're getting used to her signals. Kathleen comments about having the time to be good parents: *What else are we going to do? Let's just give up TV.* Interesting point.

Kathleen carried Joy all day. She wants to bond with her. Says she realizes the importance of that and partially credits me with helping her realize that the other day. (Anytime, dear.)

Joy soon conks out and Kathleen is not far behind.

Monday 8-24

It's been a long night. Kathleen is up three times with the baby. Joy isn't crying but she's restless, moaning, snorting — really kicking the stall. She does produce, however, another solid waste.

Joy is fussy all morning. Breakfast is a battle until she falls asleep. We eat with Lynn, another group member and single mother who has seven children. *Seven children.* Her little Alice is a picture of plump happiness.

Today Joy sports her Green Hornet jammie top, the orange blossom shorts she arrived in and her new gray/orange socks from the Times Square Mall. Later, we

> He says *One second you want to walk away and the next they melt your heart. He's got that right.*

see one of the babies in our group dressed to kill in matching hat, dress and shoes. Wow.

Joy has had the sniffles since day one and now the cold is in full swing. Rivers of mucus.

Missile crises? What missile crisis? We hear of problems between India and Pakistan. Although it's pretty heavy stuff, we sort of shrug it off. That and the latest news about Clinton's affair with Monica. I mean, we're in China adopting Joy, for heaven's sake. We're a little busy right now making our own history!

We decide to take a group trip. Joy's happy with that. It's something to do. On the bus with Martin, Number One Tour Guide, we learn more history: Sun Yat-sen led the 1911 revolution and is considered the father and founder of the Republic of China and the Nationalist Party. He overthrew the last Chinese emperor of the Ching Dynasty. He is revered by mainland China as well as Taiwan. We visit the memorial (where I visited just the other day). Nice gardens. Sun Yat-sen's statue is being refurbished and is enveloped in bamboo scaffolding. I get stopped by a Chinese guard or policeman for walking in the wrong area. That's the second time I've been chastised by a Chinese in uniform. I think about Richard Gere and his problems with the Red police in a recent movie. I had better lay low!

At the memorial we watch some straw hatted coolies

gardening. We note some purple plants like the kind in our own backyard. Interesting museum.

Later we take a bus to a silk and porcelain store. There are some very nice things. Ceramics, gold inlaid items, erotic art, carved statues of folk heroes, Buddhas. There's an artist who paints inside tiny snuff bottles, ink stamps or chop blocks and helpers scurrying everywhere.

Sun Yat-sen Memorial is probably one of the more traditional-looking places we visited in China.

We buy three lively, colorful paintings by a farmer who lives and works in the hinterland, and porcelain chopsticks. We endure a rather convoluted purchasing routine. We must place the order, have it packed and actually purchase it in three different places.

Back on the bus Joy goes absolutely ballistic. As she wails I tear off the end of the nipple on her bottle with my teeth to make a larger opening for the chunky formula. Kathleen tries to give her medication but she spits it straight up in the air and it showers someone in the seat next to us. Somehow we manage to get formula and medication down her gullet as she cries. This is the longest 15 minutes of my life.

I notice this growing wet spot on my shirt and think I'm seeing things. Soon I realize that she's peeing through her diapers.

I stay with her outside the restaurant until she falls asleep. I get encouragement from another guy in our group standing with me with his fussy child. He says *One second you want to walk away and the next they melt your heart.* He's got that right.

I'm shellshocked for a good hour. Kathleen eats with the group. *The food is really good* she says. I don't touch a thing since I feel that I'm holding a sleeping bomb — I don't want to make a move! Is it too much medication causing her tears? Not enough food? What? Folks give us their point of view. No clear cut answer.

We go back to the hotel and she makes this ride wide awake. No crying, but close to it all the way. I stand up with her as he she seems to have a problem being held while I sit. I'm so glad to get to the room. I eat peanuts and crackers from the grocery. Joy lies on the floor and plays until she falls asleep.

We make up our very own hip-hop sing-along for Joy: *She's a snot machine, she's a fuss machine, she's a piss machine, she's a munch machine* — all inspired by the rhythm and sounds of her bottle sucking, which includes slurps, kisses, spews and sighs with her guppy, rosebud lips. We think our tune is hilarious and have a

More friendly locals in the park. "Hello, how are you?"

good laugh. She just looks at us with her big, black almond eyes and nods off at last.

Monday afternoon

The three of us go to the park but we don't get far. Horribly hot and humid. People are interested in us and the baby. Four young people want us to pose with them for a photo. Imagine American kids wanting to do that!

Kathleen mixes a paste for Joy that doesn't fly. A very thick formula shake works best. I work out in the gym again on a rowing machine for 30 minutes.

Before dinner I pick Joy up and we look at our reflection in the mirror together. I notice this growing wet spot on my shirt and think I'm seeing things. Soon I realize that she's peeing through her diapers. Man, we've got to strap those things on better!

The group has dinner at the Four Seasons in the hotel. Another "fancy restaurant" according to the itinerary and indeed it is. Very good Chinese food ... for China. Drinks cost extra and the service is lousy. But Joy is a new girl this evening. Bathed, refreshed and happy. She falls asleep at dinner and goes to bed after a bottle. No fighting. What an about-face!

Everything's fine until I see the chicken head attached to the entree and that's that.

Tuesday 8-25

Joy sleeps all night. Some vocals and kicking, but nothing serious until 5 a.m. Kathleen changes and feeds her and Joy accommodates the procedure without a whimper. Both take short naps. To avoid light in the bedroom, I read in the bathroom. We go to breakfast at 6:30. Enjoyable. I load up on food. Joy is manageable (so far).

Kathleen goes to the gym. Joy gets fussy. We walk the halls but this time it doesn't do any good. I begin making a new bottle as she moans on the carpet. By the time I finish, she's asleep.

Her crying and moaning are unconvincing at times. I think she's just enamored with the wind passing through her larynx.

Joy is very congested again. More so than yesterday. I can hear it as she breathes. But she's surprisingly good-natured despite her cold.

Kathleen is becoming a Mom. She changes, feeds, plays with and thinks about her girl with an ever surer hand. I sort of fill in the gaps.

I feel slightly out of sorts. I'm developing a cough and headache.

When Joy is asleep on her back with that look of

serenity we think she's practicing being dead and lying in state.

Tuesday evening

We have dinner at a hotel near the China Hotel. Everything's fine until I see the chicken head attached to the entree and that's that. I pick at my food a little bit. Joy fusses and I take the opportunity to split with her. It's a crowded place. Many turn to look at our baby and smile. Next to our table is a wedding party. The bride is dressed in red.

We stop at McDonald's for a burger, fries and ice cream. Did I already say I hate eating this stuff? (illustrates the gastronomical bind I'm in). A young lady helps me as Joy pulls the glasses from my face. Another stops us so she can hold Joy.

Chinese tear around on bikes, scooters like this, tiny cars and buses. Everyone is going somewhere in a big, big hurry.

In our room I eat and play with the baby. I feed her some ice cream (her first taste!) Kathleen shows up and gives her a bottle. We play with her for a long time. Joy is ecstatic. We put her to bed in an amped condi-

> **Kathleen sucks out a load from one of Joy's nostrils and accidentally redeposits it in the other.**

tion but she goes to sleep. She stays down all night. I get sick during the night. I develop a painful sore throat. We are scheduled to go to the U.S. consulate tomorrow. A bad time for this.

Wednesday 8-26

As we leave breakfast, Kathleen tells me to tuck in my shirt because I'm wearing the money belt. I say the way I'm feeling I hope somebody tries to take it.

At 7:30 a.m. I go to the hotel doctor who checks me out and gives me three different medications for only 110 yuan (I thought I was going to get hit hard by the bill). He's a pleasant, older man who knows some English. The medication kicks in and I'm fine for the time being. The group loads onto the buses and we go to the United States consulate for official adoption business.

The process is painless and quick. I thought there might be a hitch because we don't have copies of our 1997 tax returns (we filed late). But no problem. While we wait, Sarah gets us water and tells us about her desire to travel abroad. She wants to visit America but apparently it's difficult to get permission from the U.S. authorities. *They think I will visit only to marry a rich American in order to stay*, she says. *Maybe someone should adopt you,* I say. She laughs.

While waiting in the hotel lobby all the group babies

After their visit to the doctor, the girls get together and compare notes.

are bunched together for a photo op. Joy stands on her head, makes a tiny A-frame with her body and brings down the house.

We go to lunch at a restaurant next to the Pearl River. I'm in no mood to eat or enjoy our meal. We bus back to the hotel and I spend the rest of the day in our room resting.

Joy is fussy early afternoon, then becomes good natured. Have we adopted a Sybil?

Kathleen and Joy's boat ride on the Pearl River that night (I'm sick in bed):
There's a kitchen on the boat and two cooks. The river is filthy. There's a deck on top with white plastic chairs. On the ride she sees new bridges, a barge with chickens and other boats that are long, low and flat with tar paper huts. She calls them floating squalor.

Along the shore are towering hotels next to ramshackle buildings. She also sees about a half dozen New England-style mansions with sprawling lawns. She's jarred to see so much space between the houses. Must be the homes of some very affluent people. The sights

> # We must cross what could possibly be the busiest, widest and wildest street in the world.

become much more pleasant at night with the lights. People wave to those on her boat.

Thursday 8-27

We wake to beating drums. There's some sort of pageant going on in a convention center across the street. Joy plays on the floor. Kathleen swings the baby and she laughs. The baby is very congested. As she naps, we hear her breath rattling through her mouth. When she wakes, Kathleen reads to her as she touches and chews the pages. Joy also likes to gnaw on sugar packets and pill boxes.

On Kathleen's first attempt with an aspirator, she sucks out a load from one of Joy's nostrils and accidentally redeposits it in the other. Oh well. Joy's cold is three days old. All the group babies are sick. Most think it's because the children are not used to the air conditioning.

I eat a full breakfast today. French toast, bacon, coffee, watermelon.

We go to the market next door to buy more medication and find none. I visit a sporting goods store that has all the latest stuff with American prices.

I have a persistent cough. Annoying. I feel sluggish. But better than yesterday.

With another couple and their child from our group,

we go to an excavation and museum about a block away from the hotel. Nicely displayed are jars, ceramic pillows, tombs and various burial items. We eat an expensive, unscheduled lunch at the China Hotel. Vegetable soup, rolls, pizza and hot tea taste very good but cost about $50.

Unfortunately, the table next to ours is seated with smokers. I wave a napkin and look over, but the three Asian businessmen haven't a clue as they chat and puff. As we pass their table on the way out, I tell them to stuff it in the simplest, crudest terms I can muster. That stops their conversation and provides us with a small chuckle.

Like father like daughter. Dad and daughter sport similar hairdos atop rather squarish heads during a visit to a museum near our hotel.

I forget I'm sick and work out too long and hard in the gym. I lift weights and go 25 minutes on the tread mill overlooking the pool. I finish just in time for a 5:30 dinner in yet another "fancy" restaurant nearby. To get there we must cross what could possibly be the busiest, widest and wildest street in the world. Cars, motorbikes and bicycles all rush toward us and stop just inches away. Again, the feeling that all walkers and riders in the streets have an invisible cushion surrounding them that prevents collision.

Martin starts pouring rice wine and the room starts to rock and roll.

On the way I talk with China Team member Lucy. She says she's 21 years old. *I say 21! You're just a baby!* She says *I'm not baby,* (pointing to Joy) *she's a baby!* Quickly changing the subject, I ask her about her career and she says that she had to study very hard to learn English. She enjoys working with parents and finding homes for the babies. She's an earnest, but thoroughly pleasant young woman.

Before we enter the restaurant we pose for a group shot underneath a mammoth billboard of the current Party Chairman. I wonder about this. Is this some sort of play on Norman's part to look good for the powers that be? Or is he in fact a true Team Player for China? If I were to ask him I'm sure the answer would be enigmatic.

The restaurant is pretty nice. Our groups get two whole rooms to ourselves. Dinner is like all the others with the Lazy Susan and all the various courses. I'm occupied with Joy, who is fussy. A lady who seems to be in charge of the banquet sees my predicament, snatches Joy and tells me her clothing's too tight and that her formula isn't hot enough. I snatch the baby back and tear away from our host and the gaggle of women who start to surround us. Joy and I settle into a quiet corner, I remake the formula and she finally takes it.

Meanwhile Martin starts pouring rice wine and the

Our group was combined with another for a total of 24 families. That's 24 babies on buses and planes. Think about it.

room starts to rock and roll. After many drinks and toasts he turns on some thumping disco. Parents hit the floor with their kids and dance. There are monitors playing videos along with tunes that include word prompts so people can sing along. *She's got it! Yeah baby she's got it! I'm your venus, I'm your fire and your de-si-re!* It's a romp and we all get into it. Joy is asleep in her Snuggly as we bop along. She wakes after a while and smiles at the party spinning around her.

Very touching and heartfelt overtures from the China Team tonight. Martin is magnificently high and dances with everybody. He tells me I have a beautiful wife and baby. I clap him on the shoulder and tell him he's a good man. Our China Team ladies sing a song, as do Jimmy and Martin. Sarah is sweet, caring and smiles a lot. Kathleen hugs her and both have tears. Even Norman gets into it with commentary and dancing. These folks perform their work with big, big hearts. This trip would not have happened without them. Navigating through the logistics, arrangements and red tape without the China Team is unthinkable.

> **Trip home is hellish. There is no comfort to be found.**

We finally leave around 9:30. Joy is pumped after the dancing. In her crib she rustles about and makes all the Joy noises. In bed that night, I cough and cough. I relapse big time. I take too much medication and stay buzzed until early morning.

Friday 8-28

We get up, prepare Joy and eat breakfast. This morning Joy goes through a symphony of sounds that include cries, coos, yelps and growls. I've got a nasty, nasty cold. Tired. Coughing. What a drag. It's hard to believe time's up. I think about what must be done back home. I had forgotten. This trip has been such a blur. We've been at the China Hotel one week today.

I think of Joy's fever, the shot, Sarah's visit and expression of duty, jogging in Yang Dong, the flat tire, coolies in the fields with their oxen, Joy's scrolls, the Park, the storm, getting lost, Chinese girls holding our baby, the awful China smell, the heat and humidity, the arctic air conditioning, our first look at Joy in her official photo *(If you don't want see, we put hand over picture)* and in-person, one mother's cry of joy to see her daughter for the first time, Norman telling caretaker to take baby back *(I not ready yet!)*, VOG: Voice of Martin *(Thisa voice of Mar-teen)*, Norman's directives *(You do this now! Don't be late!)*, Sarah saying *But it is my duty!*, Lucy saying *I'm not baby! That is baby!* Kathleen dancing in ecstasy with a sleeping Joy in her arms at the farewell party ...

Friday afternoon/night
I feel poorly but run 25 minutes on the tread machine
anyway. I have a tinny taste in my mouth and a frizzy
feeling in my face. If I've lost weight, it's in my face.
Man, I wish I wasn't sick. We
finally get packed.

The final lunch in the Four
Seasons is a bust for me. I
leave to take a last photo
shoot in the park. I'm wasted
and must drag myself around.
I'm sweating and moving in
slow motion. I take photos in
the sculpture garden and
some on the street. There's
thunder but no rain. Lots of
friendly looks. I head back at
3:30 p.m.

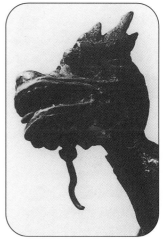

This guy wards off the evil
spirits at the Buddhist
temple we visited. We
could have used him on
the return flight.

We go to the lobby at 4:30 to
check-out and board the bus.
We say goodbye to the China
Team at the airport. Grace cries. Lucy solemnly shakes
our hands, Kathleen tears up. Sarah hugs us both.
Sweet, sweet people. We wait in various lines. There's
crying babies, sick people and everyone is tired. We're
glad to finally get seated on the plane. Goodbye, China.

Trip home is hellish. No comfort to be found. My
cough is especially bad. Joy is either asleep or all over
the place and unhappy. She wiggles and frets on our
laps. Changing and feeding her is an ordeal. In the rest
room, Joy pees between diaper changes and it gets all

We're euphoric to breathe LA air!

over Kathleen, the sink and floor. We sit next to a young Chinese boy and his father who don't seem to mind our crying baby or the score of babies around them. Amazing. Kathleen and the boy strike up a friendship and play cards.

We sweep into Los Angeles about 5 p.m. Our inner clocks are turned inside out. We're euphoric to breathe LA air! It's so sweet compared to the pea soup of Guangzhou. So happy to greet LA weather! Despite the 95 degree heat, it's nothing compared to the hot and heavy air of southern China. Our line bogs down at customs for 90 minutes, but then we finally pop through. Our friend Jim is waiting for us with camera and camcorder. He's very interested in  our baby and trip. I shuttle off to find our van. I return 30 minutes later to retrieve everyone and luggage. We decide to meet Jim for dinner in Long Beach.

To no one's surprise I order a burger, fries and a chocolate milkshake. Something as simple as that and available anywhere, anytime in the United States is a dream come true to me now. Jim shoots some footage in the parking lot. I start the drive home, but get wobbly and must pull over. Kathleen takes the wheel and makes it home as I go in and out of consciousness with Joy asleep in my lap. I'm really spaced from medication, the flu and the trip.

We get home at midnight with a sudden burst of energy. We wash the dogs, unpack a little and get to bed at 2:30 a.m.

Joy wakes at 5 a.m. We're home and it's a new life.

Just enough hair for pigtails (Spring 1999)

The first moment ...

Chapter Six:
The New Life

Actualities of having a child to care for.

The high of coming home with our own child has lasted. Perhaps the sharp thrill went away after a month or two, but the wonder of it still manages to survive even on the worst days. She is a healthy, happy, good-natured little girl and the fact remains that having her has filled out and colored our lives.

A short history

Joy was 10 months old when we got her. Right now she's 22 months old.

We came back with Joy in late August, 1998 and for the rest of the year rode out what we thought was a honeymoon period. (Looking back, however, I think it was more of an ordeal than it had to be — Kathleen and I were riding

... almost one year later.

the happy wave of Parenthood breaking upon the shores of Blissful Ignorance.)

Day care woes
By December the seams in our little Ship of Joy were starting to split because day care wasn't particularly reliable. As a result, I wasn't getting enough work done and Kathleen was having a hard time getting out of the house in the morning. We decided to shop around for a new and better service.

Fortunately indeed, we found it the first day we looked and practically in our own neighborhood. Norma's Child Care is a small, in-home service run by a licensed Child Care Provider and Board Member of the San Diego County Family Child Care Association. We spend $440 each month for care from 7 a.m. to 5 p.m. and that includes two meals a day. Almost overnight our major problems were solved. I got Joy to day care by 7 a.m., Kathleen was free to prepare for her workday, I was free to work a full 8-10 hours a day and Joy had found a wonderful second home.

It wasn't until after we had settled in with the new day care and schedule in January that I began to see how bad things had been for the first three months. It all centered around our initial day care provider and our misfortune to trust an unprofessional service (our next door neighbor). As stated earlier, we spent $1000 each month plus food and diaper costs for weekday care from *around* 7 a.m. to *around* 3 p.m. Although our neighbor had good intentions, kept a journal and provided honest care and affection for Joy, she didn't possess the reliability, accountability or professionalism we were looking for.

Mystery rash and Dr. Coldfinger
We scheduled a visit to a pediatrician soon after arriving home (the U.S. consul suggests resting for a week first). Joy had only one health problem and that was a flaming red rash that covered her cheeks and her diapered area.

The rash mystified everyone, including our doctor who actually said *We don't know much about Chinese babies.* (It took us a

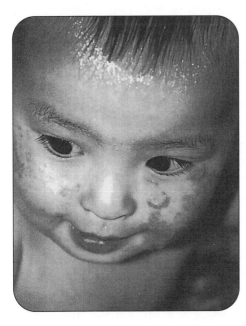

while, but we finally figured this particular MD was out to lunch. We would call him Dr. Coldfinger because every time he entered the room Joy would burst into tears — then in a droning, patronizing voice he'd have the audacity to say *When babies cry it's customary to bounce the child on one's knee to improve their disposition* — as if his walking dead bedside manner had nothing to do with it.)

He did correctly diagnose the rash as a yeast infection and to his credit prescribed a medication that cleared up the diaper rash, but her cheeks remained inflamed.

We were stymied until Bob Smith (our gardener and seasoned father of adopted children) suggested we use Aveeno, an over-the-counter skin lotion that had worked on his young son, Josh who had more or less the same problem. The oatmeal-based lotion cleared the problem almost overnight.

This and the crack about Chinese babies prompted us to fire Coldfinger and take up with a more suitable choice. Joy's current doctor is a warm and friendly Indian (Asian) woman who seems to be a much better match for Joy and us.

Coughing, sneezing, runny nose ...

The worst thing about having a baby is suffering from the sniffles so often. Day care is a breeding ground for every illness floating through the neighborhood. Joy gets sick, I get sick and Kathleen gets sick. I would estimate that I've had some sort of bug at least 20 percent of the time we've had her.

The sicknesses are of the cold and flu variety: head and body aches, runny nose, coughing, sneezing and fatigue. There doesn't seem to be an end to these bouts of illness. We haven't built up an immunity and they last for at least a week, sometimes much, much longer. One of us usually has something at any given time. I wish I could prescribe a remedy, but I don't believe there is one. Kathleen takes vitamins and supplements and there's the bit about rest and drinking fluids, but I think when you get it, you simply have to ride it out. From what I understand about viruses, there's really nothing you can do to prevent or cure them.

The colds and flus seem to strike hardest against Kathleen and me. Although Joy gets sick, it doesn't slow her down much or even affect her mood. Despite the coughing and the rivers of mucus streaming down her chin, Joy is a remarkably vigorous and upbeat little person.

Mongolian Butt?
Our girl is also very pretty and well propor-tioned. She has a purple stain on her butt that's called a Mongolian Spot, but we're told it's common in Asian babies and that it will go away in time. Other than the aforementioned rash and sniffles, there hasn't been any health problems (OK,

I forgot about the teething and her self-inflicted lumps) — certainly nothing major. We've been very lucky and I think all the parents in our group came away with equally healthy children.

Neighbors, friends and family
One of the perks of having a new child is the warmth that comes your way from neighbors, friends and fami-lies. Everybody loves babies and they bring out the best in people. We have neighbors we hardly knew come over with toys, gifts and, of course, advice. The latter is OK sometimes, annoying sometimes and something we

Kathleen and Joy share a seat with grandparents Red and Ann Werner.

eventually learned to take in stride. Even from relatives.

Friends become friendlier and families are simply over-joyed. Especially the grandmothers who had thought that they would never have grandchildren. One of the sweeter results of adopting Joy has been the delight that she has brought to Grandmothers Ann and Genie. Sure, Grandfathers Red and Gene are happy, too, but it isn't the same genetically induced euphoria. Maybe guys need the idea to sort of grow on them a bit.

Bringing home the baby has expanded and enhanced most of our relationships with others and the only sticking point has been the aforemen-

Grandparents Genie and Gene Wheeler flank daughter and granddaughter.

tioned unsolicited advice that pops up occasionally. But as we gain confidence with child rearing (or at least Joy tending), we simply don't hear (or listen to) it as much.

Fellow Adoptive Parents

Obviously, those who have adopted from China share a unique and special experience. In particular, you can expect to enjoy a close bond with members of your China group. I get e-mail updates almost every day about legal matters, parenting and reunion plans. It has become a rich and vital resource.

You will also discover new friendships with others in your hometown who have adopted from China. Perhaps there's even a local chapter or organization you can get in touch with.

Days in the Life

Day-to-day: Mornings

On workday mornings Joy gets up around 6:30. She wants to be with Kathleen and may want a bottle, but eating isn't her priority right now. She wants to be with Mommy.

At 7 I take her to child care. She is happy to go and happy to be dropped off. Her caretakers are loving and professional. Her playmates are within a year or two of her age and Joy loves playing with them. She gets at least two meals a day at day care and may not even need to be fed in the evening. The kids play in the house and back yard. There's some structure but not a whole lot. They do learn to play and interact with each

Our China Group's first reunion (August 1999).

other in constructive ways. Every Monday I show up with a week's supply of extra clothing, diapers and wipes along with a check for $110 (make no mistake — it's the bargain of all time).

Day-to-day: Evenings
On workday evenings I pick up Joy at 5 and I have her until Kathleen comes home at 6:30. We play with each other and she usually takes a bottle during that time period. Sometimes she wants close interaction with me and sometimes she's happy on her own.

When Kathleen comes home, I hand Joy off. Kathleen likes to feed her something in her booster chair, play with her and later on read to her. At 7:30 or 8:00 Kathleen begins to prepare Joy for bed by putting her into her jammies.

In the winter putting Joy to bed is easier because it's darker and quieter in general. In the summer it's more difficult because of the longer days and the extra excitement that warm weather seems to bring. Sometimes we have to go through a concerted ritual of reading, then turning out all the lights and the TV. One of us picks her up and quietly walks her around the dark house and into her bedroom. She's ready to be placed in her crib by 8 in the winter and probably a little later, say 8:30, in the summer.

There are difficult times when she may need to be driven around in the car or van, stay up longer or simply left screaming in her crib with pillows over our heads. The latter does not happen often, of course, and can usually be traced to a specific problem, like staying up too late the night before, illness, teething or demonic possession.

Day-to-day: Weekends and holidays
Without day care she's ours all day long. Kathleen is in charge and I'm frankly very happy about that. When Kathleen needs to do something on her own, however, I take over. We try to do something as a threesome each free day we have her and that may include walks, shopping trips and visits to the park, zoo, beach or our friends' homes.

She enjoys the hustle and bustle of public places, the company of other people and new sights and sounds. She's often cranky if we make no plans and just hang around the house. In other words, just relaxing is out of the question. She needs stimulation.

Car rides are OK if they last only an hour or so. She enjoys the scenery passing by but not being strapped in. Some of her worst tantrums have occurred on the freeways and it's because she hates confinement.

She used to nap a lot, but at 22 months she's going down only once a day between 11:30 a.m. and 1 p.m.

It's important that she sleep at that time or she won't sleep at all and that could be trouble.

This leads to the importance of consistency, which is built into the work week and day care system, but not necessarily into the weekends or holidays. Kathleen and I are spontaneous by nature and must think hard about feeding and allowing for naps when it's our responsibility. Not that we ever forget to care for her, but we may miss a feeding or sleeping window by 30 minutes because we're on the move. And that may result in an unhappy Joy.

Summaries

Kathleen and I have been on a learning curve and there has been more than one bad moment, but it's getting better. It's a matter of acceptance and better planning.

My bad times are usually about me not accepting Joy as a child. If I start thinking she should be doing something she isn't capable of — like taking care of herself so I can go surfing, or sitting still so I can enjoy a meal, or cleaning up after herself — then I'm in trouble.

There's a special way to deal with children and for Kathleen and me that has been new territory since we simply haven't had the experience. To be honest, we are also older, somewhat set in our ways and more selfish than we usually care to admit.

Kathleen's New Life

Joy has been with us for almost a year now. What is it like having her in our lives? It is utterly transforming.

One cannot have a child and expect anything to ever be the same. I underestimated the depth of the adjustment we would have to make. I thought that I could certainly handle changing diapers, bathing, feeding, dressing and preparing a baby for bed at night. Beyond being prepared for these parenting chores, I eagerly anticipated reading to her and simply holding her.

What I didn't count on was the discombobulated feelings I would have at work. It is true that, at least at first, a new parent loses his or her edge. There is no doubt about it — sleep deprivation combined with the stress of juggling career and parenthood makes the job suffer. I suppose parents who have a full-time, live-in nanny may not have this problem, but that is not the case for us. We have used a baby sitter only a handful of times, and that means that when I am not working or commuting, I am attending to her full-time, and that takes a lot of energy.

But the challenges of instant parenthood are quite separate and apart from Joy herself. She is healthy, beautiful, responsive and robust. Joy has none of the attachment disorder that we had read about and feared we might have in a child who started life in an institu-

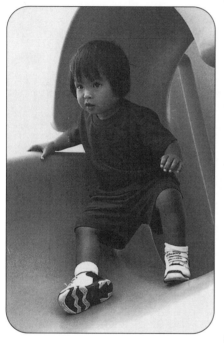

tion. Quite the contrary, she protests vigorously when we leave and she is warmly receptive and responsive to our affection.

In spite of the rough patches, it still seems like a miracle that we have Joy in our lives. It has been a long and winding road — through the decision making process, the year of adoption procedures culminating in the trip to China, the return home and the transition to a new way of life — but it has also been an exhilarating ride. The wonderful part is that we have been blessed with an adorable child.

Chapter Seven:

One Year Later

August 13-15, 1999
San Mateo, California
Of the 24 children who were adopted in our group last year, 22 showed up with their families for the first reunion. Most remarkable is how healthy, robust and pretty every girl is after 12 months of TLC from their new parents.

Many of the kids were once listless, somber and pale. The only thing vibrant about them were their cries. But after just one year our children are vigorous, happy and glowing.

If there's sure-fire testimony concerning Chinese adoption, it certainly was there that weekend. Can you imagine that these girls were ever abandoned? Can you believe that there are millions of children like these in orphanages still?

Appendix: What other adoptive parents think

Six families in our group generously answered questions about their experiences with the adoption. Their thoughts should prove helpful to prospective parents.

Answered by:
a. Jamie, Mary Ann and Elise
b. Randy, Toni and Katie
c. Brad, Kim, Nicole and Cassandra
d. Roy, Terrie and Rachel
e. Becky and Tori
f. Mark, Carolyn and Lea

1. What were your reasons for wanting to adopt a child?

a. We couldn't physically have our own and we always felt we had a lot of love to share with a child.

b. Randy and I wanted to experience parenthood just like everyone else. We had tried (unsuccessfully) for several years to have a child. We had investigated private domestic adoption, but found the hoops (with no guarantees) more than we were willing to endure.

c. We couldn't have children and it was more important to parent than to keep trying to have a child.

d. We wanted to have children and be a family. Whereas Roy and I are good friends and have a great marital relationship, something was missing. It wasn't important to us if the child was ours biologically or what "race" she was. We just wanted to love a child and help her to grow up with a strong sense of self-esteem and family values. We thought we were both emotionally, physically and financially in a good position to offer this to a child.

e. I have always wanted to be a mother (since I was 13 or 14). But, since I haven't found "Mr. Right," I wasn't able to have the traditional family. I have always felt that there were many children that needed homes. After I finished law school and passed the bar exam, I checked into adopting in San Bernardino County. I went through their homestudy program, and that solidified my resolve to adopt, although due to other circumstances, I chose to adopt from China.

f. We're in our mid-40s and since I can't have biological kids, we decided to adopt.

2. If you are married, to what extent did both you and your spouse have equal commitment to the adoption?

a. I would say that I was 100 percent and Jamie around 50 to 60 percent.

b. Toni initiated the process (her biological clock was winding down) and was committed from the very start. She made the phone calls and filled out the forms. Even now any legal forms (Social Security, birth certificate, citizenship) are completed by her. I became truly committed to the adoption when I finally met Katie. I think I had to see her before she became a reality.

c. Both of us were ready and open to adoption.

d. I had basically decided that adoption was a good alternative for me, so I had to introduce Roy to the concept and let him become accustomed to the idea. We talked to several people, both men and women, who had already done this and the feedback was very positive, which I think helped Roy become more comfortable with the idea. I let Roy think about it for about a month with no pressure and when we discussed it, Roy was very open to the process.

e. Not applicable.

3. What was your greatest concern in adopting a child?

a. My greatest concern (and this is a little selfish) was that the child would be either mentally or physically handicapped or emotionally scarred from being abandoned.

b. Our ability to be good parents and to provide a child with the love, support and guidance that she would need.

c. Questions she will have about her birth parents. We plan on taking our girls back to China when they get older. That and having no information on her medical background.

d. Her health of course! We're not too worried about explaining to her about her birth or why she was adopted.

e. Whether I was being fair to a child, knowing that the child would not have a father. However, I felt much better about taking a child who needed a home than conceiving one. I felt that a one-parent family would be better than a no-parent family. Sometimes I still worry about that, but there are several male figures in Tori's life. Who knows, maybe I'll meet "Mr. Right" someday!

4. What did you most look forward to in adopting a child?

a. I looked forward to having someone to carry in my arms and to feel that they needed me as much as I needed them.

b. Sharing our life and love with a child.

c. Being a family.

d. Teaching her things, singing songs, playing games, helping her with her homework, visiting grandma, helping her to grow up into a loving, giving, gracious woman who is confident in herself, everything we would have looked forward to with a biological child. We realize Rachel is "adopted" but it's really just a word, she is our daughter in every sense of the word.

e. Nurturing a child and being a mom. Just being a family.

5. What were your reasons for choosing to adopt a Chinese child?

a. We chose a child from China because of Jamie's heritage, but also because of the overabundance of female babies readily adoptable. I had asked about children from Ireland and Poland because that is my heritage, but because of the religious factor (they are usually Catholic) they keep their babies and tend to have large families.

b. We fit the Chinese adoption profile and we have other Chinese relatives married into the family. We feel comfortable with the ethnicity and culture.

c. Mother is Chinese and the children from China are known to be healthy.

d. I knew someone wasn't going to come after her in six months and want MY baby back, as I have heard has happened in the U.S. Also, I thought that the general health would be better with a Chinese baby than one from the former Soviet Union. She was only "abandoned" because she was a girl and not for any health (physical or emotional) reasons.

e. I originally did not consider adopting internationally due to the cost. I did attempt to adopt through the county. I was assigned a 6-year-old girl and we started the transitional process. After that agreement, I was advised of serious mental problems suffered by this child. At that time the placement terminated because as a single parent I did not feel I could give this child the attention she needed (luckily, she has now been placed with a two-parent family). I had considered China at one point, but because of the age limits, I was too young. When I turned 35, I started the process. I had learned a great deal about Chinese orphanages through various television programs.

f. Mark and I decided on China because we wanted a healthy baby girl and we knew China almost guaranteed that. We decided against local adoption because of the law that favors birth mothers.

6. What was the most difficult aspect of the adopting procedure?

a. It was difficult to wait after the paperwork was finished, but actually it wasn't so long!

b. The homestudy was the most difficult because we felt that our agency did not keep in contact with the social worker and much time was wasted. It was very frustrating. Also, the waiting time once our paperwork was submitted to the child program. We realize that the agency went as quickly as they could, but the waiting was very stressful.

c. The long wait with no answers.

d. The paperwork! And the wait. And the unknown. Looking back, it really wasn't that bad or long, it just seemed that way. As we've just finished the dossier for our second adoption, we're more organized with what is needed and we know more about the process.

e. The wait! Not knowing when you're going and the details of our daughter. I was NOT a very good waiter.

7. What was the most positive aspect of the adopting procedure?

a. The trip was so well organized and the wonderful families we got to meet and be connected with.

b. The support given by the other adoptive parents during the time in China as well as this past year.

c. When they put our daughter in our arms.

d. Our daughter finally being ours to hold and love. Also all the people we've met and how supportive our families and friends have been. And being able to share our experience with others who are just beginning to think about adoption, especially from China.

e. What was the most positive? The acceptance of my daughter by my family and friends has been amazing! She is just plain part of the family, which is great!

f. It has been the most positive experience for both of us and we have a wonderful child on top of all the pluses. We have gained an incredible extended family, too. We are big-time advocates to everyone we meet. We suggest that they do the same thing we did, whether or not they have a child/children. We have given advice to many couples already and two are starting the process with Norman! We are exhausted but extremely happy and have absolutely no regrets.

8. What was the most difficult aspect of your trip to China?

a. I would say the language barrier. It is not so easy just to run out to a store to buy something as simple as a teething ring!

b. The flight over. Waiting, waiting, waiting. The heat/humidity. Self-induced stress.

c. The shitty plane ride on China Southern! Felt like cattle in a barn. We once flew Cathay Pacific and they had plenty of walking room. The food was better as well as the service.

d. The travel, the plane ride, the time/jet lag. The lack of fresh fruit, the humidity, the heat (these last two are because of the time of year we traveled). I wish we had been able to do a little more sightseeing, but I was ready to go home as soon as we got Rachel.

e. What was the most difficult aspect of our trip to China? The heat! I do not do well in the heat. I also got sick for a few days and that was very difficult with an 8-month-old. Luckily, I had two travel mates who pitched in and took care of Tori.

f. Weather problems and possibly food issues, but that would apply even in the USA!

9. What was the most positive aspect of your trip to China?

a. Again I would have to say the organization of all the

official papers, plans and the daily routine.

b. The guidance, organization and support given by the placement agency.

c. When they put our daughter in our arms.

d. Meeting other families who were in the process with us, supporting us and being supported by us. Meeting the China Team who were all so nice and willing to help out whenever they were needed. Seeing how another culture lived and appreciating more the things we take so much for granted here in the U.S.

e. What was the most positive? Besides getting Tori, I LOVED the group we traveled with. I know that I made lifelong friends for Tori and me on the trip. I feel it is very important to stay in touch with those who adopted from the Yangchun orphanage. I feel it will be important for her later in life to know others who came to families the same way she did. Three or four families from Southern California have gotten together every couple of months who adopted from Yangchun. I feel that is very important.

f. The trip was the most well organized we've been on, and we've travelled extensively.

10. What is the most difficult aspect of rearing your new child up to now?

a. I feel as if I need a lot more energy and time in a day. Elise has actually been a great kid so far so I haven't run into too many difficulties!

b. There was a language barrier for six to eight months before we truly knew that we were understanding each other.

c. None.

d. Patience on my part. But I'm learning. Not picking her up every time she cries or whines but still being there for her, understanding her needs. Being unable to comfort her when she's teething or has a fever when I can't explain to her why she's in pain or hurting.

e. Having to work is difficult. I think that my daughter is thriving, but I wish I could work less and be with her more. Also, just being a new mom is tough, but we're doing just fine.

11. What is the most positive aspect of rearing your new child up to now?

a. The most positive has been to see her grow, gain weight and reach her age-specific milestones at the approximate age. Her laugh and smile are very positive for us!

b. When she called us Mama and Daddy and truly knew what that meant.

c. When they put our daughter in our arms.

d. Her calling me mama, responding to my "I love you" with her "I love you." It just makes my heart sing with happiness. There's a love I had never before been able to imagine. Taking her little hand and walking with her, teaching her things along the way about flowers, cats, slides, airplanes, picking blackberries and so many little things that I hadn't really given that much thought to. Singing lullabies to her at night when she's having difficulty sleeping. Seeing her interact and play with Roy. Knowing that she trusts us and relies on us to protect her.

e. I love having Tori to go home to (even on the fussy nights!). I love seeing her develop. It is amazing that when I got her she couldn't even sit up and now she's talking and running!

12. To what extent are you involved in actively preserving your child's Chinese heritage?

a. Jamie's mother speaks Chinese to her, she often eats Chinese food, I read some Chinese books and stories to her and we have Chinese artwork displayed throughout our house!

b. We have done very little because of the language barrier, but now we are purchasing books of Chinese folk tales and Chinese cookbooks.

c. We are carrying on the same Chinese traditions as we have always done in my family.

d. Not so much now, but as she gets older, I want her to know games that Chinese children play and what life in China is like.

e. I get together with those who adopted from Tori's orphanage and I am involved in Families with Children from China (FCC). I feel that as Tori gets older, we will try to be involved in more, but at this age, all she does is play with other little girls. I think it's important for her to know that there are other families just like ours.

Glossary

Adoption: The transfer of all parental rights and obligations from one person or couple to another person or couple through legal means.

Adoptive parents: An individual or couple who have chosen to adopt and have received court approval.

Birth child: A parent's biologic child.

Birth parent: A child's biologic parent. Also bioparent.

Finalization: Involves a court date where the adoption is finalized and parents receive an adoption decree.

Foster parents: An individual or couple who has temporary care of a child. Unlike adoptive parents, they have no legal rights in determining many aspects of a child's life.

Homestudy: The preparation, study and investigation by a social worker of the family who wishes to adopt. A homestudy includes visits to the home, interviews and background checks on financial, health and criminal records.

Homestudy agency: The agency licensed in your state to fulfill the homestudy required by state law *(see Homestudy).*

Immigration and Naturalization Service (INS): The agent of the United States federal government that oversees the adoption process to make sure that the child is coming here legally, that the family is aware of the process and that the family can take care of and be responsible for the child.

International child program: The agency approved by the Chinese government that finds your child (called the child referral), handles the adoption procedures in that country and arranges your travel and accommodations while you are there.

Mongolian spot: Harmless purple-colored spot often found on the skin of Asian babies.

One-son/two-child policy: China's current policy of population control. Families are restricted to conceiving one male child; if the first child is female, they may legally give birth to one more child.

Post-placement: Visits to the home by a social worker after the child has been placed with a family.

Re-adopt: The legal process of obtaining a birth certificate in the United States for an internationally adopted child. The child was adopted in the country from whence he or she came and now must be adopted in the United States, hence re-adopt.

Special needs: For Chinese adoptions, refers to children with physical, emotional or medical disabilities.

Waiting period: The period after a family is approved for adoption by an agency until a child is placed with them.

Resources

Books

Adoptive Families of America
Parenting Resource Materials
3333 Hwy. 100 North
Minneapolis, MN 55422
612-535-4829

China Books & Periodicals, Inc.
2929 Twenty-fourth Street
San Francisco, CA 94110
415-282-2994
Fax 415-282-0994
email info@chinabooks.com
www.chinabooks.com

Faraway Lands Book Market
PO Box 662
Dixon, IL 61021-0662
800-556-3645
email fraway@essex1.com
http://www.adopting.com/
faraway

Tapestry Books
Adoption Book Catalog
PO Box 359
Ringoes, NJ 08551-0359
800-765-2367
Fax 908-788-2999
www.tapestrybooks.com

The Heritage Key, Inc.
6102 East Mescal
Scottsdale, AZ 85254-5419
602-483-3313
Fax 602-483-9666

Database

National Database of Children
Adopted from China
Christian World Adoption
270 West Coleman Blvd.
Mt. Pleasant, SC 29464
803-856-0305

Magazines and newsletters

Adopted Child (newsletter)
PO Box 9362
208 South Main Street, #3
Moscow, ID 83843
email: Lmelina@moscow.com
http://www.raising adopted
children.com

Adoptive Families Magazine
Adoptive Families of America,
Inc. (AFA)
2309 Como Avenue
St. Paul, MN 55108
800-372-3300

*Holt International Families!
Magazine*
Holt International Children's
Services
PO Box 2880
1195 City View
Eugene, OR 97402
541-687-2202
Fax 541-683-6175
email: info@holtintl.org
www.holtintl.org/

Ours
Adoptive Families of America
3333 Hwy. 100 North
Minneapolis, MN 55422
612-535-4829

Organizations

AASK America/
Adopt a Special Kid
657 Mission Street, Suite 601
San Francisco, CA 94105
415-543-2275

Adoptive Families of America
2309 Como Avenue
St. Paul, MN 55108
800-372-3300

Adoptive Families of America
(AFA)
3333 Highway 100 North
Minneapolis, MN 55422
612-535-4829

American Academy of Adoption
Attorneys
Box 33053
Washington, DC 20033
202-832-222

Children Awaiting Parents (CAP)
700 Exchange Street
Rochester, NY 14608
716-232-5110

The Institute for Black Parenting
9920 Lacienega Blvd., Suite 806
Inglewood, CA 90301
310-348-1400

Joint Council on International
Children's Services
7 Cheverly Circle
Cheverly, MD 20785
301-322-1906

National Adoption Center

1500 Walnut Street, Suite 701
Philadelphia, PA 19102
800-TO-ADOPT

National Adoption Foundation
100 Mill Plain Road
Danbury, CT 06811
203-791-3811

National Adoption Information
Clearinghouse
10530 Rosehaven, Suite 400
Fairfax, VA 22030
888-251-0075

National Council For Adoption
(NCFA)
1930 Seventeenth Street, NW
Washington, DC 20009
202-328-1200

National Council for Single
Adoptive Parents
Box 15084
Chevy Chase, MD 20815
202-966-6367

North American Council on
Adoptable Children
970 Raymond Avenue, No. 106
St. Paul, MN 55114
612-644-3036

Resolve Inc.
(Infertility support group)
310 Broadway
Somerville, MA 02144
617-623-0744

U.S. Department of Health and
Human Services (HHS)

200 Independence Avenue SW
Washington, DC 20201
202-619-0257

Private Agencies
Adoption Services International
2021 Sperry Avenue
Suite 41
Ventura, CA 93003
805-644-3067
Fax 805-644-9270

Family Connections Adoptions
PO Box 576035
Modesto, CA 95357-6035
209-869-8844
Fax 209-869-7334
email: famconnadopt
@earthlink.net

Holt International Children's
Services
PO Box 2880
1195 City View
Eugene, OR 97402
541-687-2202
Fax 541-683-6175
email: info@holtintl.org
www.holtintl.org/

U.S. Asian Affairs
539 E. Garvey
Monterey Park, CA 91755
626-288-2220
Fax 626-288-2378

Vista Del Mar
3200 Motor Avenue
Los Angeles, CA 90034
310-836-1223
Fax 310-836-3868

**State Adoption Agency
Listing**
State Agencies for all fifty states
plus Washington D.C., Puerto
Rico and the Virgin Islands.

Alabama Department of Human
Resources
205-242-9500

Alaska Department of Health
and Social Services
907-465-3170

Arizona Department of
Economic Security
602-542-2362

Arkansas Department of Human
Services
501-682-8462

California Department of Social
Services
916-445-3146

Colorado Department of Social
Services
303-866-3228

Connecticut Department of
Children and Youth Services
203-238-6640

Delaware Department of
Children, Youth and Their
Families
303-633-2655

District of Columbia
Department of Human Services

202-727-3161

Florida Department of Health
and Rehabilitative Services
904-488-8000

Georgia Department of Human
Resources
404-894-4601

Family Court (Hawaii)
808-548-4601

Idaho Department of Health
and Welfare
208-334-5700

Illinois Department of Children
and Family Services
312-814-6864

Indiana Family and Social
Service Administration
Division of Family and Children
317-232-4420

Iowa Department of Human
Services
515-281-5358

Kansas Department of Social
and Rehabilitative Services
913-296-4661

Kentucky Cabinet for Human
Resources
502-564-2136

Louisiana Department of Health
and Human Services
504-342-4086

Maine Department of Human
Services
207-287-5060

Social Services Administration
(Maryland)
410-333-0219

Massachusetts Department of
Social Services
617-727-0900 ext. 565

Michigan Department of Social
Services
517-373-3513

Minnesota Department of
Human Services
612-296-3250

Mississippi Department of
Public Welfare
601-354-0341

Missouri Department of Social
Services
314-751-4832

Department of Family Services
(Montana)
406-444-5900

Nebraska Department of Social
Services
402-471-9331

Special Needs Adoption,
Division C&FS, Nevada
Department or Human Services
702-486-7800

New Hampshire Department of
Health and Welfare
603-271-4677

New Jersey Department of
Human Resources Division of
Youth and Family Service
609-984-8202

New Mexico Human Services
Department
505-827-4058

New York State Department of
Social Services
518-473-0855

North Carolina Department of
Human Resources
Division of Social Services
919-733-3801

North Dakota Department of
Human Services
Child and Family Services
701-224-4805

Ohio Department of Human
Services
614-466-9274

Oklahoma Department of
Human Services
405-521-2475

Oregon Department of Human
Services
Children's Services Division
503-378-4452

Pennsylvania Department of

Public Welfare
Office of Children, Youth and
Families
717-787-7756

Puerto Rico Department of
Social Services
Office of Child Services and
Community Development
809-723-2127

Rhode Island Department of
Children and Their Families
401-457-4548

South Carolina Department of
Social Services
Office of Human Service and
Self Sufficiency
803-734-6095
800-922-2504

South Dakota Department of
Social Services
605-773-3227

Tennessee Department of
Human Services
615-741-5935

Texas Department of Human
Services
512-337-3422

Utah Department of Social
Services
801-264-7589

Vermont Department of Social
and Rehabilitative Services
802-241-2131

Virginia Department of Social
Services
804-662-91331

Administration for Children,
Youth and Families
Department of Human Services
St. Thomas, Virgin Islands
809-774-7865

Washington Department of
Social and Health Services
206-753-3478

West Virginia Department of
Health and Human Resources
304-558-7980

Wisconsin Department of
Health and Social Services
608-266-0690

Wyoming Department of
Family Services
307-777-6789

Support Group
Families with Children from
China (FCC)
Call information for the
chapter nearest you.

Web sites
Find several useful links at
www.adoption.com.

Bibliography

Adopted Child. Various issues. Moscow, Idaho.

Adoption Services International. Various materials. Ventura,
California.

Adoptive Families Magazine. St. Paul, Minnesota: Adoptive Families
of America, Inc.

Family Connections Adoptions. Various materials. Modesto,
California.

Hi Families. Eugene, Oregon: Holt International Children's
Services, Inc.

Money Magazine. New York, New York: November 1997.

New Choices Magazine. April 1999.

Thomas, Dave. *Adoption Works for Everyone: A Beginner's Guide
to Adoption.* 1990.

Index

Adoption procedure 35-46
Adoption Services International (ASI) 12

China Hotel 24
China Team 25-26
China trip and journal 56-103
    Buddhist temple 85
    Bus trip back to Guangzhou 75-76
    Bus trip to Yang Dong 66-67
    China Hotel 60
    Chinese adoption agency 64-65
    Flight back 101-102
    Flight over 58
    Guangzhou 59-69, 75-101
    Park 81-82
    Receiving our children 68-69
    Shopping 77-78, 84-85, 89
    Sun Yat-sen Memorial 88, 89
    Traffic 79
    United States consulate 94
Costs 21-32
    Airline fees 24
    Explanation of fees 23-26
    Homestudy fees 23
    Hotel and meal costs 24
    Immigration and Naturalization Service (INS)
    fees 24
    International child program fee 25-26
    List of fees 22-23
    Orphanage donation 25
    Post-trip costs 31-32
    Trip costs 27-30
Cowie, Nancy 37

Day care 48-49, 106
Decisions about adopting 9-20
        Good and bad reasons to adopt 12-13
        Kathleen's decision 17-20
        To adopt 11-14
        To adopt from China 15
        To adopt internationally 14-15
        To have a child 9-11

Emotional upheavals 50, 51

Family Connections Adoptions 22, 23, 40
First months: a short history 105-116
        Day care 106
        Health issues 107-109
        Kathleen's new life 115-116
        Mongolian spot 109
        Rash 107
        Relationships 109-111
        Typical daily routines 111-114

Health issues 107-109
Hicks, Sandie 36
Homestudy 36-42

Immigration and Naturalization Service (INS) 22, 24, 37-38, 42
International child program 23, 25-26, 36-37, 43-44

One year later 117-119
Orphanage 22, 23, 25
        Girls in Chinese orphanages 16-17

Post-trip costs 31-32

Preparing for a child 47-55
        Day care 48-49
        Emotional upheavals 50-51
        Things to buy 51-52

Re-adopt 23
Reasons to adopt 12-14
Relationships 109-111

Summary of costs 32

Tax break for adoptive parents 32-33
Trip supplies 27-30
Typical days 111-114

What other adoptive parents think 121-132
        Commitment 122-123
        Concerns 123-124
        Difficulties rearing new child 129-130
        Difficulties with adoption procedure 126
        Difficulties with China trip 128
        How they preserve heritage 131-132
        Reasons for adopting 121-122
        Reasons for adopting in China 124-125
        What is positive about rearing child 130-131
        What they looked forward to 124
        What was positive about adoption procedure 127
        What was positive about China trip 128-129

About the Authors/Parents

Doug Werner is the author of all ten books in the Start-Up Sports series — a series of sport instructional guides. *Adopting in China* is a chronicle of his first foray into the extreme sport of parenting.

Kathleen Wheeler/ Werner works in the field of Human Resources and Development. She holds a doctorate in psychology and needs it to live with Werner (her husband) and to mother their supercharged adopted daughter, Joy.

The Werner family lives in Chula Vista, California, just outside San Diego with their two cairn terriers, Billy and Lulu.